Arts & Crafts

Arts & Crafts

IN BRITAIN AND AMERICA

Isabelle Anscombe & Charlotte Gere

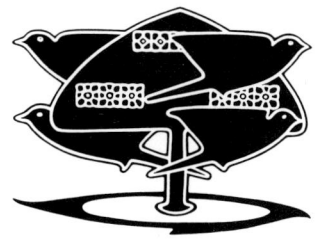

RIZZOLI

ACKNOWLEDGEMENTS

We would like to acknowledge the generous help of Alan Crawford, Arthur Grogan of Standen, East Grinstead, David Allen Hanks, Clive Wainwright and Michael Whiteway. For their help in obtaining the illustrations we thank Victor Arwas of Editions Graphiques Gallery, London; Keith Baker of Phillips Fine Art Auctioneers, London; Mary Comino of Cheltenham Museum; Shelagh Ford of The American Museum at Bath; Howard Grey; Louis H. Kohlenberger of University City Library; Mrs Langlands of the Bethnal Green Museum, London; The Metropolitan Museum of Art, New York; Ian C. Monie of the Glasgow School of Art; Eudorah C. Moore of California Design; Christopher Payne of Sotheby's, Belgravia, London; Jessie Poesch of Newcomb College; Peyton Skipwith of The Fine Art Society, London; and the staff of the photographic department of the Victoria and Albert Museum, London. We are also indebted to Miss Felicity Ashbee for granting permission to quote from her father's letters and journals, and to Mr. P.J. Croft of King's College Library, Cambridge.

Frontispiece
Philip Webb – Staircase at 'The Red House', 1859.

Front cover
C.F.A. Voysey – 'The Wykemist'.
Fragment of a carpet made by
Tomkinson and Adam,
Kidderminster, 1897.

Back cover
Frank Lloyd Wright – Stained glass
window from the Dana residence,
Springfield, Illinois, 1902.

First published in the United States of America in 1978 by
Rizzoli INTERNATIONAL PUBLICATIONS, INC.
712 Fifth Avenue/New York 10019

Library of Congress Catalog Card Number 78-58700
ISBN: 0-8478-0184-5

Printed and bound in Hong Kong

CONTENTS

INTRODUCTION

The Arts and Crafts movement of the 19th century compounded many different aspects of the design, modes of production and politics of its time. As a movement, it can be seen both as a political struggle against the encroachment of industrialism on the workman's way of life and as a decisive change of style within the decorative arts. The origins of the movement have been traced from the Government Reports on design and industry of 1836, the Great Exhibition of 1851, 'Summerly's Art Manufactures' and the mediaevalism of Pugin, Ruskin and Morris. However, the total field within which the movement grew was far more involved than such landmarks in its development suggest.

During the nineteenth century an awareness had developed that national style reflected the moral values of a society: if a society was unable to produce good design then the fault lay in its ethical system — a nation's art was a symptom of its moral health. The Arts and Crafts movement combined this feeling with its own social aims, finding a perfect symbolism in the return to mediaevalism. Fine craftmanship was never in jeopardy, but the need for 'an English art for England', culminating in the adoption of Gothic as the best national idiom, gave the men of the Arts and Crafts movement, the majority of them architects, the necessary representation of a popular art and allowed them, in rejecting more traditional historical styles, to bring art back to the people whom their political aims supported. Their furniture reflected in concrete form the way of life of the craftsman, stressing the honesty of production with structural features becoming often the focal point of the decoration. 'Fitness for purpose' became an element of style, and although the same principle was held by designers whose work was machine-made, in the Arts and Crafts doctrine 'purpose' was defined in relation to everyday life among the woodshavings and smell of resin, in the silvershop or blacksmith's, and not to the world of industry, commerce and 'laisser-faire'. As William Morris wrote in a letter of 1883, explaining his espousal of the socialist cause:

> . . . I do not believe in the world being saved by any system, — I only assert the necessity of attacking systems grown corrupt, and no longer leading anywhither: that to my mind is the case with the present system of capital and labour: as all my lectures assert, I have personally been

1 C.F.A. Voysey. Printed cotton for G.P. and J. Baker, c. 1897.

gradually driven to the conclusion that art has been handcuffed by it, and will die out of civilisation if the system lasts. That of itself does to me carry with it the condemnation of the whole system, and I admit has been the thing which has drawn my attention to the subject in general.[1]

In 1855 Matthew Arnold had written of 'Two worlds, one dead or dying, one struggling, but powerless to be born.'[2] In many ways almost every aspect of Victorian life was divided into two such worlds: north or south, capitalists or working men, education or the enforcement of strict codes of duty, religion or new scientific discoveries and theories. In such a world the importance of finding a symbol of national unity and cohesion became paramount. To the Victorian critic there was seldom a choice to be made in the face of such dichotomies; the question lay in finding the right elixir to bind both sides together into a coherent whole, whether it be Newman's Catholicism, the 'sweetness and light' of the 'culture' of Matthew Arnold, Pater's Platonism or the mediaevalism of Pugin and Ruskin. To many it seemed that progress, sanctified by evolutionary ethics, must eventually solve its own ills. Indeed the Government Reports of 1836 had set out to do just that in the area of design; Britain led Europe industrially but could not compete economically if production was artistically inferior. The Report pragmatically set out to discover what was wrong and to remedy it, not least through the setting up of the Schools of Design. But critics such as Newman ridiculed the notion that 'education, railroad travelling, ventilation, drainage, and the arts of life, when fully carried out, serve to make a population moral and happy'[3]; ridiculed the notion that all that was needed was a factual investigation.

The work of the firms which exhibited at the many International Exhibitions of the latter part of the century testified to the continuing existence of fine craftsmanship. Pugin, Talbert and Godwin designed for firms such as Crace, who exhibited in London in 1851 and in Paris in 1867, Holland and Son exhibiting in 1855 and 1862, Jackson and Graham, 1851, 1862 and 1872, James Lamb of Manchester, 1862, W. Smee and Sons 1862, Gillow, 1851 and 1862, Collinson and Lock, 1871, Hardman or Hart and Son. Antiquarianism was a dominant influence on design: '. . . at the present time it may be said that in almost all European countries not only Mediaeval, but Renaissance and all the more modern styles, are produced in furniture with more knowledge, taste and skill, than they have been for a long period.'[4] The furniture at the Great Exhibition was condemned for its lack of taste but not entirely for the attempt to copy past styles, as Owen Jones' *Grammar of Ornament,* published in 1856 demonstrated: William Morris had a copy in his library. However, for the first time importance was given to the familiar and domestic design of the nation; the aristocratic patronage of art had given way to the domination of art in the middle class home.

1 William Morris, a letter to C. E. Maurice, Kelmscott House, 1 July 1883. Quoted in J. W. Mackail's *Life of William Morris*, 1899, Vol. II, p. 106.

2 Matthew Arnold, 'Stanzas from the Grande Chartreuse', 1855.

3 Newman, 'Liberalism', *Apologia pro Vita Sua*, p. 501.

4 Yapp, Art Industry, *Furniture, upholstery, and house decoration, c.* 1878–80, Shoreditch District Library.

2 Matthew Digby Wyatt and Owen Jones in the Open Colonnade of the Crystal Palace at Sydenham, 1853-4.

To a large extent this insistence on national design must have been due to the all too obvious miseries of industrialisation, a somewhat hypocritical 'cover-up' operation as well as a very real concern to improve the working and living conditions in the fast growing industrial towns, where medical reports laid the blame for rampant disease on degraded housing and social investigations condemned squalor as a factor in crime and immorality. The Schools of Design had indeed provided a step forward in national art teaching, but were necessarily linked to the economic demands of machine production rather than to any particular educational ends: it was the gentlemen of the Arts and Crafts movement who were to begin to realise the aims of artistic education for the working man. But it was, to begin with, an attempt to unify, to provide some cohesion in the life of the working man rather than to fully support the demands of working class organisation which were having devastating effects abroad.

The French Revolution and the escalation of working class agitation were seen as the results of a lack of spiritual guidance among the working class population. Carlyle had set the tone in *Chartism* of 1839:

> What are all popular commotions and maddest bellowings, from Peterloo to the Place-de-Grève itself? Bellowings, *in*articulate cries as of a dumb creature in rage

3

and pain; to the ear of wisdom they are inarticulate prayers: 'Guide me, govern me! I am mad and miserable, and cannot guide myself!' Surely of all 'rights of man', this right of the ignorant man to be guided by the wiser, to be, *gently or forcibly**, held in the true course by him, is the indisputablest.

To dispel the 'darkness, neglect, *hallucination'** which were the result of that original industrial unrest the working men were to be given guidance and reassurance. The image of guidance which was to gain the most powerful hold on the popular imagination of the age was a return to the values of a mediaeval society. Both Ruskin and Pugin, though differing in their religious affiliations, saw the mediaeval workman as the model of contentment and creativity. Such a return to the implications of feudal authority and religious autonomy were to provide the framework for the right of the working man to be governed by the man of letters, the sage, the seer, but such a solution was at best merely a reassurance that the 'dumb creatures in pain' would be taken care of.

Go forth again to gaze upon the old cathedral front, where you have smiled so often at the fantastic ignorance of the old sculptors: examine once more those ugly goblins, and formless monsters, and stern statues,

3   The Socialist League, Hammersmith, *c.* 1885. The group includes William Morris, his daughter May and Emery Walker.

*my italics

10

4

5

4 Richard Norman Shaw – Oak bookcase with inlaid decoration, 1861.

5 C.L. Eastlake – Library bookcase.

anatomiless and rigid; but do not mock at them, for they are signs of the life and liberty of every workman who struck the stone; a freedom of thought, and rank in scale of being, such as no laws, no charters, no charities can secure; but which it must be the first aim of all Europe at this day to regain for her children.[5]

So wrote Ruskin oratorically in 1853, precisely directing the gaze away from the men for whom he claimed protection and towards the art produced. It is this assumption, that because the art of that time was praiseworthy so equally the society must have been just and happy and worthy of re-creation in his own age, that caused the constant repression of recognition of the true victims of Victorian social unrest and misery and allowed Ruskin's writings to enlist the sympathetic imagination of an age which wanted nothing less than the emancipation of the working classes.

So too could Pugin define the 'rights of hospitality' of mediaeval times in relation to the architecture and conclude

5 Ruskin, 'The Nature of Gothic', *The Stones of Venice*, 1853, p. 14.

that 'Catholic England', by which he meant mediaeval England, 'was merry England, at least for the humbler classes; and the architecture was in keeping with the faith and manners of the times, — at once strong and hospitable.'[6] Both Ruskin and Pugin stressed the importance of decorative schemes for public buildings which would set an example to those who saw them and reassure those who felt a lack of coherence in society by their external coherence, which symbolically marked the state's authority. In such a way the manifestations of the Gothic Revival, such as Pugin's designs for the Houses of Parliament, did help to give England a more secure identity, but always remained somewhat distant from those who lived in the shadow of the mills or factories (which provided the financial strength for such buildings), supplying those people with only a 'mirage philosophy'. Ruskin wanted, through art, to bring man closer to nature and to his own soul, but in many ways such ideals could only hope to instil the aims and morals of his class into the working man, giving him the spiritual base he required, by giving him what were inevitably only the same leisure pursuits.

In 1854 the Christian Socialist F. D. Maurice founded the Working Men's College in the East End of London. He had earlier started co-operative stores in the poor and densely populated areas of industrial England, giving the people an idea of the benefits of systematic co-operation among themselves, and he had himself taught and lectured at the 'Hall of Association', the central London branch. The Working Men's College grew out of this experiment, partly inspired also by a 'People's College' started in Sheffield in 1842 and by the school of design opened for mechanics by the painter Thomas Seddon, where Ford Madox Brown had taught. Ruskin immediately interested himself in the project and taught a class in drawing and design, encouraging the artists D. G. Rossetti and Madox Brown to teach there also. They were joined by Edward Burne-Jones, Arthur Hughes, Stacey Marks, Lowes Dickenson and others. There were also lectures on science, history and art. More colleges were gradually opened in towns where there were already co-operative stores. Maurice declared that 'A Working man's College must assert the principle that God is to be sought and honoured in every pursuit, not merely in something technically called "religion".'[7] This practical Ruskinianism of Christian Socialism led Maurice to much pioneering work, not least in the education of women.

The other educational institution set up for the working man was the pioneer university settlement of Toynbee Hall. There the young Cambridge graduate C. R. Ashbee was the only architect on the staff and we have his own accounts of 'grand old Morris in his peacock blue shirt as bluff and powerful as ever'[8] lecturing on behalf of the Socialist League and of his own visits to speak in halls in the poor and squalid districts of London, recruiting working men for his Ruskin reading class.

6 A. W. N. Pugin, *The True Principles of Pointed or Christian Architecture*, 1841, p. 61.

7 F. D. Maurice, quoted in A. H. Mackmurdo, *History of the Arts and Crafts Movement*. Typescript, William Morris Gallery, Walthamstow, Essex.

8 C. R. Ashbee, unpublished letters and journals, King's College Library, Cambridge. By kind permission of Miss Felicity Ashbee.

6 Edward Burne-Jones – Caricature of William Morris giving a lecture on weaving, c. 1886.

The flamboyant figures of the Pre-Raphaelite artists must have been strange spectacles to the East Enders and they themselves must have learnt much from practical contact with the working classes. Among Ashbee's papers is this letter from one Fred Hubbard in 1887:

It would delight me very much if I could be of any service to you in the art class you write of, but I am afraid you are mistaken in me in consequence of my having been egotistical and boastful that evening we were alone at Toynbee. May I tell you some truth about myself? . . . I left school at fourteen after receiving a very poor education — was excessively fond of trying to draw — parents poor so in view of 'respectable' after life I became an office-boy — (they did not want their children to work hard). Loose companions for five years or so nearly made a Whitechapel Rough of me — a book or two saved me from it — but I know nothing, having read little but Dickens, and him but imperfectly. My greatest fear is of developing into a 'man of business' — crafty and dishonest — I grope to find a way out of it, but cannot . . . Do you really think such a one as I could be of use to you?

A. H. Mackmurdo, in the Preface to his *History of the Arts and Crafts Movement,* wrote: 'The more extensive our vision; the more intensive our sentiment, the greater appears the human importance of this movement' and, further, that he saw the movement 'not as an aesthetic excursion; but as a mighty upheaval of man's spiritual nature' in an attempt to throw off the materialism of the age. What many of the leading Arts and Crafts designers were to find was that their struggle became a fight for the continuing financial independence of the way of life they championed. Morris & Co., despite its original conception lying in Morris' own desire for simple well-made furniture for his Red House, continued to produce decorative items and schemes for the rich, such as St. James's Palace or Jesus College Chapel and Queens' College Hall at Cambridge. Peter Floud has pointed out that even for the more domestic or middle-class items produced by Morris & Co. the actual method of production was more suited to the machine, the hand-blocking of wallpapers or chintzes being in fact extremely monotonous and requiring no individual expression from the craftsman.[9] Morris himself thoroughly enjoyed his experiments with weaving or dyeing, but for the company to survive economically certain compromises had to be made. One of the shareholders of Ashbee's Guild of Handicraft wrote to Ashbee in 1907, when new funds were needed for the Guild to continue, that he had 'had a little experiment last year in selling several large pieces of furniture made by Morris & Co. The result showed that there is no general public for such things, each individual piece is made for an individual buyer, and probably if Morris & Co. had to make such things for stock they would soon be in the same hole as you are. They

9 Peter Floud, 'William Morris as an Artist: a new view' *The Listener*, 7 and 14 October 1954.

have as the result of a longer existence a considerable and more or less constant demand for certain wall papers and cretonnes, and machine-made carpets and other repeat orders where their prices don't differ much from those of ordinary commerce. Such orders don't of course solve the question of finding employment for specially trained cabinet makers, carpet makers, and metal workers, but the profit on them goes to pay the expenses at Oxford Street.'[10] The initial commercial success and survival of Morris & Co. came from their stained glass, as the experiments by Burne-Jones, Rossetti, Morris and his friends coincided with the revival in ecclesiastical building and renovation where stained glass was in great demand. As Walter Crane wrote:

> The great advantage and charm of the Morrisian method is that it lends itself to either simplicity or splendour. You might be almost as plain as Thoreau, with a rush-bottomed chair, piece of matting, and oaken trestle table; or you might have gold and lustre (the choice ware of William de Morgan) gleaming from the sideboard, and jewelled light in the windows, and walls hung with arras tapestry.[11]

There was indeed charm in such a method, but there was also economic necessity.

7 Page from Morris and Co. catalogue, c. 1910.

10 Ashbee shareholder, one of several letters quoted in C. R. Ashbee's *Craftsmanship in Competitive Industry*, 1908.

11 Walter Crane, *The English Revival in Decorative Art, William Morris to Whistler*, 1911, p. 54.

8 J.P. Seddon – Cabinet designed for Morris and Co., with scenes from the honeymoon of King René of Anjou painted by Ford Madox Brown, Edward Burne-Jones and D.G. Rossetti, 1861.

Much of the Morris & Co. furniture was in fact made in the eighteenth century manner and, despite his socialism, Morris himself was hardly sanguine about the chances of the various Guilds which were to be formed for idealistic reasons. Ruskin's St. George's Guild, founded in 1871, met with little success, though perhaps its aims were realised in a more pragmatic manner by the Cadbury village later set up in Birmingham where, if Ruskin would hardly have applauded the work, the leisure hours were 'humanised'. It is interesting to note that Ruskin's support of the Pre-Raphaelite artists, who had in many ways engendered the aims of the Arts and Crafts movement, allowed him to encourage the financial support of Ernest Gambart, the first really successful London art dealer who established Victorian art — including the work of Holman Hunt, Millais, Madox Brown and D. G. Rossetti — as a true commercial venture. Gambart had rivalled the Royal Academy in exhibiting the important pictures of his day, as Millais wrote to Effie in May 1860, that Gambart 'says if I will let him have my pictures to exhibit separately from the Royal Academy, he will give me as much again for them; it would be worth his while.'[12] It could have been with this experience in mind that Ruskin wrote to Morris in 1878, embodying the idea which was to lead to the formation of the

12 Jeremy Maas, *Gambart: Prince of the Victorian Art World*, 1975. Letter from Millais to Effie, 3 May 1860.

9

10

Arts & Crafts Exhibition Society in 1888: 'How much good might be done by the establishment of an exhibition anywhere, in which the Right doing, instead of the Clever doing, of all that men know how to do, should be the test of acceptance.' Liberty & Co., which was to espouse Arts and Crafts design, was formed in 1875, seven years before the formation of Mackmurdo's Century Guild and nine years before the Art Workers Guild. It was indeed several years before the public began to recognize the political aspects and origins of the Arts and Crafts movement. Where the changes in style wrought by the Arts and Crafts movement were most influential were of necessity, in the end, where they were commercially successful. That is why in many ways the design and the ethics of the movement now seem paradoxical. The movement was the inspiration both of social change and of designers as varied as Louis Comfort Tiffany, Christopher Dresser or Gustav Stickley. Above all it created an atmosphere where personal ideas could be encouraged. It is with these diffuse influences in mind that it is fascinating to look at the importation of Arts and Crafts across America.

9   Isaac E. Scott – Walnut bookcase inlaid with various woods, 1875.

10   Philip Webb – 'Clouds'. Interior of the house designed for the Hon. Percy Wyndham, 1881-6.

11   Philip Webb – Firegrate, fender and fire irons in a panelled surround, 1894.

12 Morris and Co. – Mahogany table, standing on a Morris carpet, bowl by William De Morgan.

From the end of the eighteenth century America had had its own perfect example of the Arts and Crafts ideal in the Shaker communities in New York State. 'Mother' Ann Lee had emigrated to New York with eight other Shakers, or Shaking Quakers, from the slums of Manchester in 1774. She died in 1781, but under the leadership of Joseph Meacham new communities were founded, separate from the world and preaching equality of the sexes, spiritual purity and honest craftsmanship in everything they made. In 1852 a chair factory was founded to make furniture for outside sale, its principles based on the ideals of 'regularity is beauty' and 'beauty rests on utility'; an ironic comparison to the judgements on the Great Exhibition of the previous year in England. By 1870 the New Lebanon, New York, settlement was thriving financially, selling healing herbs, farm machinery and buildings, and furniture. In 1845 Friedrich Engels, though rejecting their religious beliefs, had cited the Shakers as proof of the possibility and practicality of Communism and their productions emphasised the conviction that the utility, simplicity and perfection of their environment constituted a moral obligation within their communities, reflecting their spiritual practices. By 1860 their vernacular had become fashionable on the East Coast but by the time that English Arts and Crafts ideals were being followed in America the Shakers' influence was on the wane.

The growth of industrialism, with means of communication widening and the development of a greater national awareness, meant, as it had in Britain, that there was a concern for a national formulation of style. The American Institute of Architects had been founded in New York as late as 1857 and most architects were still dependant on European styles, although Frank Furness in Philadelphia and H. H. Richardson in Boston did much to develop new styles. Between 1890 and 1910 the number of American architects studying at the Ecole des Beaux-Arts in Paris was at its peak. During the 1860s the leading furniture designers were centred on the East Coast, such as Isaac Scott who produced Gothic pieces after the British movement, or Herter Brothers of New York, who worked with H. H. Richardson, making pieces with elements of both Gothic and Queen Anne styles before successfully absorbing the new Japanese taste. One of the most popular influences on American taste came about through the publication of Charles L. Eastlake's *Hints on Household Taste*, first published in England in 1868. Eastlake advocated Gothic designs, although he admitted to a greater eclecticism than adherence to one strict idiom would generally allow. However, in 1878, in the Preface to the book's fourth edition, he was moved to write that he found 'American tradesmen continually advertising what they are pleased to call "Eastlake" furniture, with the production of which I have had nothing whatever to do, and for the taste of which I should be

13 Reconstruction of a Shaker room.

very sorry to be considered responsible'. Meanwhile, at the various International Exhibitions of the mid-nineteenth century American exhibits were mainly praised for their technical virtuosity, such as the American Revolving Spring Chair exhibited in 1851 by the American Chair Company of New York. In 1876 European styles were still slavishly and anachronistically copied and the Philadelphia Centennial Exposition of that year provided a lesson on the lack of good American design. However, it also provided an invaluable showcase for new European techniques and idioms, especially in ceramics, with exhibits from Royal Doulton, Sèvres and from Japan. Between that exhibition and the Chicago World's Fair of 1893 America showed an enormous step forward in the quality of her design.

In Philadelphia itself the leading cabinet maker was a German, Daniel Pabst. At the Centennial Exposition he won an award for a sideboard, despite some subsequent criticism: 'The amount of rich carving far surpassed that on any other Gothic piece in the Exhibition; but in the main it was without purpose or distinctive meaning. Still it was free from conventionalisms . . . Mr. Pabst also displayed a Renaissance sideboard, which however has few merits as compared with his

14 Landing in Gustav Stickley's house at Craftsman Farms.

13 'Daniel Pabst — Philadelphia Cabinetmaker' by David A. Hanks and Page Talbott, Philadelphia Museum of Art *Bulletin*, April 1977, Vol. 73, No. 316, p. 21.

Gothic work. His Gothic work reflected the prevalent defects of the revival in the tendency to introduce too many architectural forms pertaining to stonework only.'[13] This criticism compares badly with the exhaustive reports prepared by the organisers of the Great Exhibition of 1851 in England. There, despite the enthusiasm and efficiency with which the nation had organised the building of the Crystal Palace and the displays within it, the artistic exhibits were almost without exception condemned as 'indolent and servile', indiscriminate copies of other unsympathetic or alien cultures. Crass over-decoration had prevailed, with allegorical scenes depicted on every type of household object. The reports summed up what had been learned from this unfortunate display of bad taste: the use of narrative designs was firmly condemned and conventionalised observations of nature encouraged, with greater attention to strict botanical fact. Matthew Digby Wyatt concluded with what were to become the central tenets of the Government Schools: 'We have now arrived at a recognition of the four principal elements which invariably concur in producing those emotions of delight, which may be regarded as infallible tests of our contact with real beauty in the productions of Nature — Variety — Fitness — Simplicity —

15

16

15 Dr. Christopher Dresser –
Electro-plated soup tureen and ladle
made by Hukin and Heath, design
registered 28th July 1880.

16 W.A.S. Benson – Copper and
brass chafing dish and stand, the dish
electro-plated inside, *c.* 1895.

17 Archibald Knox (attrib.) –
'Cymric' silver bowl with a lid and a
spoon designed for Liberty and Co.,
c. 1903.

18 Rex Silver (attrib.) – Silver vase,
1901.

17

18

and Contrast.'[14] The Americans had not yet formulated such quasi-scientific principles of aesthetics.

Daniel Pabst had been influenced by English Gothic designers such as Bruce Talbert, but after the Exposition his work showed a decided change, with severer lines and conventionalised motifs, which could only have stemmed from the work of Christopher Dresser. Dresser had visited Philadelphia that year on his way to Japan and lectured at the new Pennsylvania School of Industrial Art, where another British silver-designer, Archibald Knox, was to lecture thirty-six years later. He had entered Somerset House, the first of the Schools of Design, in 1847 and held a doctorate in Botany, his work being an extension of Goethe's theory of metamorphosis; an associate of Owen Jones, the champion of conventionalisation and eclecticism, Dresser designed for industrial production and held to a strict functionalism with the theory that good design should reflect the presence of 'mind', of secular scientific knowledge, particularly botanical fact. 'True ornamentation is of purely mental origin,' he wrote, 'and consists of symbolised imagination or emotion only.'[15] Such scientifically elegant theories must have been a revelation to the American labouring under the debt of European domination of style, especially the freedom such theories allowed in their insistence on secular design, on adherence to national characteristics in the present and no longer to past traditions with their old loyalties. In this way Dresser's theories were revolutionary and even departed from the Arts and Crafts ethic which supported design tied to a certain cultural value. Such a sudden impact of new thought upon an already established and successful furniture-maker demonstrates the authority with which British craftsmen and designers were heard in America at that time.

There was much contact between the two sides of the Atlantic towards the end of the nineteenth century. In 1882 Oscar Wilde undertook an eighteen month lecture tour of the United States, advocating the Aesthetic ideals lampooned in Gilbert and Sullivan's operetta *Patience* which opened in New York during his visit, only five months after its London première. Oriental goods had been exhibited at Philadelphia and Wilde's hugely successful tour made the Aesthetic adoption of Japanese motifs more widely popular and advertised the sunflower and lily, the emblems of that ideal. Wilde, for all his decadence and élitist poses, was concerned for individualism in art and took interest in the social ideals maintained by the Arts and Crafts movement. His remarks must have opened the way for a freer and more flamboyant attitude to art in what was a rather conservative market.

The next major English figure to visit America, at a time when contact was established in many fields, not only art, was Walter Crane. An exhibition of his work which was to tour America with him had been financed in its freightage from England by the Boston Museum of Art and he paid his own

14 Matthew Digby Wyatt, Society of Arts, Lectures on the results of the Great Exhibition of 1851, 1852–3, Lecture XIX, p. 223.

15 Christopher Dresser, 'Ornamentation Considered as High Art', a paper read before the Society of Arts, 10 February 1871.

19 Charles Sumner Greene – Teak armchair made for the Blacker house, 1909.

20 Gustav Stickley – Reclining oak chair made in the Craftsman Workshops, *c*. 1905.

21 Liberty and Co. – Reclining armchair, *c*. 1905.

22 Morris and Co. – Adjustable armchair adapted from a design by Philip Webb, *c*. 1865.

expenses during the trip by commissions executed in America. He arrived in Boston in 1891 and met with a rather cool reception after he spoke in support of the Chicago Anarchists at a memorial service at Paine Hall. The Anarchists had been condemned to death after a bomb went off among police waiting to break up a meeting of strikers in Chicago in 1887; Crane's speech was reported in the press and subsequently he was banned from several clubs and a dinner to be given in his honour had to be cancelled. Crane had been introduced to Socialism by W. J. Linton during his apprenticeship as a draughtsman at Smith and Linton, commercial wood engravers, and had been finally persuaded by William Morris who had introduced him to H.M. Hyndman and Prince Kropotkin at the Social Democratic Federation, where he also met Dr. Aveling and Eleanor Marx. He had corresponded with Morris on the subject and wrote that: 'The result was that the difficulties disappeared, and from the verge of pessimism as regards human progress, I accepted the Socialist position, which became a universal solvent in my mind.'[16] Crane joined Morris' Socialist League and later the Fabian Society (whose meetings Oscar Wilde attended upon occasion) and had designed cartoons for *Justice* and *The Commonweal,* covers for *Time* and *The Practical Socialist* and also for a song written by Morris to be sold in the streets at the funeral of Alfred Linnell. Linnell had been killed on 'Bloody Sunday' at the rally in Trafalgar Square on November 13th, 1887 held in protest against the Government's support of the sentences given to the Chicago Anarchists.

Crane was surprised 'in what I had supposed was a free country'[17] to meet with such condemnation for his sentiments. He had already suffered mild persecution for his views when Sir Coutts Lindsay, a director of the Grosvenor Gallery in London, had progressively been unwilling to hang his pictures, which dealt with socialist themes. In 1887 he had been forced to withdraw *The Riddle of the Sphinx* which had been hung behind a pillar in the corner of the corridor. However, he had more support in London, for the Grosvenor Gallery subsequently closed and the other directors formed the New Gallery where the first Arts and Crafts Exhibition Society show was held the following year. But Crane continued throughout his American trip to be more interested in the condition of American labour than in architecture or art. In Boston, although he noted with approval the excellent collection of Japanese artefacts in the Art Museum, he was more intrigued to meet Edward Bellamy, the author of the socialist utopia *Looking Backward*. The exhibition of his work toured Boston, Chicago, St. Louis, Philadelphia and Brooklyn and he spent five weeks in Chicago where he lectured at the Art Institute and then went on to Los Angeles and San Francisco. In New York he met the stained glass designer John La Farge and Will H. Low and designed a wallpaper and frieze, incorporating Columbus' ship and the Stars and Stripes, for

Opposite
23 Ford Madox Brown – 'The Marriage of St. Editha and Sigtrig, King of Northumberland', stained glass panel, *c*. 1873.

Page 28
24 Henry Holiday – Stained glass panels depicting the Annunciation to the Virgin, *c*. 1890.

16 17 Walter Crane, *An Artist's Reminiscences*, 1907, Chapter VIII.

17 Ibid.

the forthcoming Chicago World's Fair. In Philadelphia he was interested to meet Mr. Gompers, the President of the American Federation of Labour, and discuss the progress of the movement and was disappointed to miss a scheduled mass labour demonstration. It was perhaps due to his priority of interest that his visit did not seem to provoke such reactions in the decorative arts as did C. R. Ashbee's later visits.

Within America itself the most important diffuser of Arts and Crafts ideals was Gustav Stickley of Syracuse, New York State. He had been trained as a stonemason and furniture-maker and then in 1898 he visited Europe, meeting C. F. A. Voysey, Ashbee, Samuel Bing and others, after which he returned to Eastwood, Syracuse, not only to establish his own workshops but also, beginning in 1901, to begin the publication of *The Craftsman* magazine. In the first issue of *The Craftsman*, which was a monograph on William Morris, he wrote that his 'United Crafts endeavour to promote and to extend the principles established by Morris, in both the artistic and the socialistic sense.' In 1904, in 'Thoughts occasioned by an anniversary', he wrote of his return from Europe that 'In America, as I looked about me with a clearer, keener vision than ever before, I recognized that the salvation lay . . . with the workers, rather than with the possessors of hereditary culture, or of immense wealth and the power attendant upon it. I realized that the twentieth century, then a few years distant, was to be, like the thirteenth, distinctively an Age of the People.' The second issue of *The Craftsman* was an appreciation of Ruskin; in such a way did he acknowledge his debt to the British movement. In America he wanted to establish a truly democratic art. For the first two years, when his two brothers were employed, he experimented with a Guild system, but it proved to be financially unrealistic, and for the first few years of *The Craftsman* he encouraged socialist writers to contribute, such as John Spargo or A. M. Simons, editor of the *International Socialist Review*. Among the articles were pieces on 'Homeless England', 'Social Work in British Factories', Jack London, Dr. Barnardo, Morris' socialist articles from *Justice* such as 'Work in a Factory as It Might Be', as well as on Indian Missions or the Bromsgrove Guild, Rodin, J. S. Henry, or Art Nouveau, described as 'wilful and somewhat dangerous tendencies' in European art.

The Craftsman did more than any contemporary magazine in America to publicise the Arts and Crafts ideals; indeed, 'craftsman' became an accepted word for a certain basic quality and style in furniture. Some of Stickley's designs are similar to Morris & Co. designs and Stickley supplied plans in the pages of his magazine for his own designs to be followed by would-be craftsmen. In 1903, in the catalogue to an Arts and Crafts exhibition held in Syracuse, Stickley set out his principles of design:

They are, briefly stated: the prominence of the structural idea, by which means an object frankly states the purpose

Page 29
25 Edward Burne-Jones – Detail from a stained glass window, showing an angel with a harp, c. 1880.

Opposite
26 William De Morgan – Panel of thirty-six tiles, designed by William Morris for Membland Hall, Devon, 1876.

for which it is intended, in the same way that a building, architecturally good, reveals in its façade the plan of its interior. The second characteristic . . . is the absence of applied ornament, of all decoration that disguises or impairs the constructive features. The third is the strict fitting of all work to the medium in which it is executed; the development of all possibilities of color, texture and substance; the choice being dependant upon the beauty, without regard to the intrinsic value of the material employed.[18]

In the 1904 article quoted earlier he had written that:

The very crudity of my structural plan, as I apprehended it, was to me a proof of its vital power, as well as of a promise of progress, because *formlessness* never follows hard upon crudeness; because also decadence is the natural sequence of over-refinement.[19]

Stickley's designs were in many ways crude and certainly included little decoration, honesty to the wood, usually oak, being the main consideration. In his writings he stressed the importance of the ethics of good design having an influence on the consumer as much as on the maker and seemed to espouse a quasi-psychological explanation of how poor design influences the state of society in which it is produced. 'Non-structural objects, those whose forms present a chaos of lines which the eye can follow only lazily or hopelessly, should be swept out from the dwellings of the people, since, in the mental world, they are the same as volcanoes or earthquakes in the world of matter. They are creators of disorder and destruction. The shapes of things surrounding the working members of society should carry ideas of stability and symmetry in order to induce a correspondence of thought in those to whose eyes they present themselves. They should not picture the world in a state of flux.'[20] The world which should be presented was a democracy; practical art should be taught in preference to the history of the development of design which would tend to detract from the present age. By 1906, in an article on 'The Use and Abuse of Machinery' in which he championed the use of the machine in furniture production, and incidentally about the time when he no longer encouraged socialist articles in the pages of *The Craftsman*, he wrote that

. . . the hope of reform would seem to be in the direction of a return to the spirit which animated the workers of a more primitive age, and not merely to an imitation of their method of working . . . the real friendliness of machinery to the handicrafts would be shown in the growth of an industrial art as vital and lasting as that of the mediaeval craftsman toward whose methods of work it is now the fashion to cast such longing eyes.

In terms of the creating of a democracy through its expression in the material productions of society, Stickley was here echoing Frank Lloyd Wright who also insisted that a true American style must be founded upon a present which

27 Frank Lloyd Wright – Oak table made for the Darwin R. Martin house, Buffalo, 1904.

18 Gustav Stickley, 'A Recent Arts and Crafts Exhibition held in the Craftsman Building, March 23, Syracuse', *The Craftsman*, Vol. IV, May 1903.

19 20 Gustav Stickley, 'Thoughts Occasioned by an Anniversary', *The Craftsman*, 1904.

20 Ibid.

28 Rookwood Pottery –
Earthenware vase by Matthew A.
Daly, 1890.

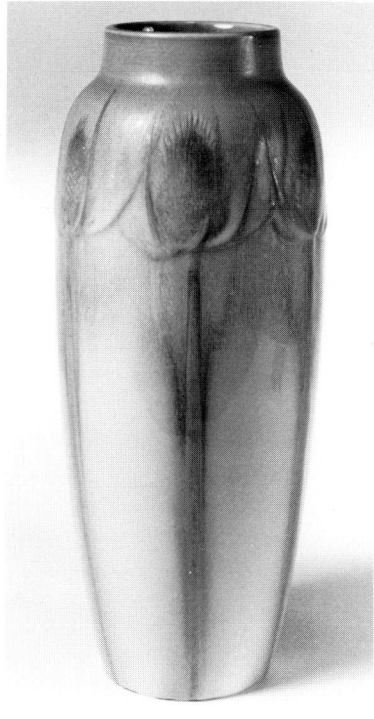

29 Cincinnati Pottery –
Earthenware vase with
underglaze decoration, *c.* 1880.

included the machine, that indeed it was the machine-age which was to be exalted. Stickley's designs, however, do not reflect the espousal of the machine but remain founded in the Gothic cathedral which had been his inspiration on his return from Europe. One is tempted to see the change in his views as more of a compromise for the financial continuance of his workshops after he had expanded into prestigious New York offices in 1905; in New York he had perhaps found more business-like and commercial attitudes than in Eastwood. Certainly he may have found that the socialist ethics expressed in *The Craftsman* were not entirely sympathetic to new friends found in the city.

By 1901, when *The Craftsman* was first published, the term Arts and Crafts had become more widely known in America, though it was Stickley more than anyone who gave it its own American flavour. In 1893 the exhibits gathered at the Chicago World's Fair had given the Americans increased confidence in their decorative arts and in December 1896 the first issue of *House Beautiful* had been published in Chicago with articles and designs by Morris, Crane, Ashbee and Voysey. This magazine had first spread the word of the Arts and Crafts movement, giving people increased knowledge of what was happening in Europe. The English *Studio* was also published in America under the title *International Studio,* disseminating English propaganda. In 1897 the first American exhibition of Arts and Crafts had been held at Copley Hall in Boston and the Boston Society of Arts and Crafts founded in June; in October the Chicago Arts and Crafts Society was founded and had 128 members within its first six months, including Frank Lloyd Wright. In 1898 there had been an exhibition of Ashbee's Work in Chicago, with a second exhibition in 1900 including Walter Crane's work. Perhaps the most widespread influence for the aims of the movement came about through the growth of art pottery in America. This remained very largely the dominion of women as various clubs and colleges were set up to provide respectable work for ladies. The Cincinnati Pottery Club had been founded in 1879, followed in 1880 by the Rookwood Pottery, in 1895 by Newcomb College in New Orleans and publicised further by Mrs. Adelaide Robineau's publication of *Keramic Studio* in 1899, which included designs and advice for would-be potters. The standard of American pottery was extremely high, so much so that by 1909 the St. Louis entrepreneur E. G. Lewis could persuade the celebrated French ceramist Taxile Doat to leave Sèvres, with many of his finest examples, for University City where a new, very fine clay had been discovered. Despite the financial failure of the venture it remains an indication of the appeal of the New World's potential.

C. R. Ashbee had first visited New York and Philadelphia in 1896, leaving unimpressed with the work he saw, but in 1900 he returned on a longer visit to lecture on behalf of the National Trust. Canon Rawnsley, a founder of the Keswick

30 Interior of L.C. Tiffany's studio in New York.

School of Industrial Art, had been to the States in the spring of the previous year and had done much towards establishing contacts for Ashbee's tour. Visiting fourteen states, Ashbee had a heavy commitment of lectures and in Washington had meetings to discuss where a headquarters for the Trust should be established, taking into account the problems of having too many organisational centres on the East Coast. Many of his lectures dealt with the social commitment behind the work of the Trust and of the Arts and Crafts movement. It is to be remembered that the political awareness in America at that time had a different basis from England, with her dependence on colonies and a more rigid class structure. The American politics rested less on questions of socialism or its repression, as Walter Crane had discovered to his cost, but more largely with the ideals of democracy, powerfully inspired by the frontier concept.

In his report to the National Trust Ashbee wrote: 'Philadelphia together with Boston [where he had lectured to the Arts and Crafts Society] and Chicago appears to me to be producing among the young men that force which with us has developed in the Art Workers Guild and the Arts and Crafts

31

32

31 Charles Rohlfs – Oak table, made for Rohlf's own home in Buffalo, c. 1902.

32 Ambrose Heal – Oak dining chair, c. 1910.

21 C. R. Ashbee, *A report by C. R. Ashbee to the Council of the National Trust for places of historic interest and natural beauty, on his visit to the United States in the Council's behalf, October MDCCCC to February MDCCCCI*, Essex House Press.

22 C. R. Ashbee: ibid. (National Trust Report).

23 C. R. Ashbee: ibid. (National Trust Report).

movement, which sets its face against Professionalism in Architecture, the force that sees in the work of the architect or the practice of his art a moral and ethical responsibility.'[21] It was by Chicago, however, that he was most impressed: 'Chicago is the only American city I have seen where something absolutely distinctive in the aesthetic handling of material has been evolved out of the Industrial system.'[22] There he addressed ten separate meetings, including the Art Institute, the Arts and Crafts Society and Hull House, which was modelled on Toynbee Hall and from the start had incorporated an art gallery and studio. A committee was set up in Chicago to consider the question of the National Trust and 'Mr. Frank Lloyd Wright, one of the leading spirits among the younger architects, and of whose work the city may well be proud, was appointed secretary.'[23]

On his last day in Chicago Ashbee visited Wright at his home; here is his own account of that visit from his Journals:

Wright is to my thinking far and away the ablest man in our line of work that I have come across in Chicago, perhaps in America. He not only has ideas, but the power of expressing them, and his Husser house over which he took me, showing me every detail with the keenest delight, is one of the most individual of creations that I have seen in America. He threw down the glove to me in characteristic Chicagoan manner in the matter of Arts and Crafts and the creations of the machine. 'My God', said he, 'is machinery, and the art of the future will be the expression of the individual artist through the thousand powers of the machine, the machine, doing all those things that the individual workman cannot do, and the creative artist is the man that controls all this and understands it.' . . . I added the rider, that the individuality of the average had to be considered, in addition to that of the artistic creator himself.

A long friendship developed from this first meeting between the two men: Ashbee and his wife visited Wright again in 1908 and 1915, Wright stayed at Chipping Campden in 1910 and they corresponded until 1938. In many ways Ashbee strongly resisted Wright's ideas about the use of the machine, although he accepted that America had to forge a new architectural and decorative style of her own, using none of the vocabulary of ancient Europe, but formulating a standard for the present, especially to fulfil the growing needs of civic development. Wright was insistent that beauty must come from the use of the machine and that it was for the artist to 'create a new beauty from apparent ugliness.'[24] Such a view tended to by-pass Ashbee's concerns with education, with the role of the worker-craftsman, with the opportunity to educate the consumer-public through good design made available and, most of all, with the priority of the well-being of the average man over the aesthetic value of the objects produced. This much had he learnt from his Ruskin reading class at Toynbee Hall. One cannot help wondering what would have been the result of a meeting between Wright and Christopher Dresser, with his emphasis on secular design and use of machine techniques. Ashbee, however, rather disliked the speed and clamour of Chicago and, as his wife Janet wrote on their second visit to the Wrights: 'Much of his building is, to me, too bizarre and away from all tradition to be beautiful; and the decoration of squares and geometric lines I find fussy and restless. But he has big ideas and is gloriously ruthless in sticking to what he believes.'[25]

While Ashbee was in Chicago in December 1900 his wife and a friend visited the Roycrofters at East Aurora, New York, where her husband had been invited to speak. They arrived in a snowstorm and were met by Elbert Hubbard, the founder of the community, who showed them excellent hospitality. Hubbard had been a successful soap-salesman for many years until, in 1892, he had visited England where he met William Morris and saw the Kelmscott Press. Upon his return to America he had published the first issue of the *Philistine* magazine on his own press in May 1895, following it with an edition of six hundred illuminated copies of the *Song of Songs*. As the press and all the associated trades of bookmaking expanded the Roycrofters began shops for the production of furniture, ornamental iron-work and china. Building their own shops and houses the Roycrofters had a plan for complete communal living, providing education and an apprenticeship

33 The Roycrofters – 'Gray's Elegy: A Lyric Poem'. Hand-illuminated book in browns and blues with black lettering outlined in gold, designed by Samuel Warner, 1903.

24 Quoted by Janet Ashbee (letters and journals in King's College, Cambridge).

25 Janet Ashbee: C. R. Ashbee, unpublished letters and journals (King's College, Cambridge).

34 Roycroft Shops – Oak magazine rack, c. 1912.

system, organised lectures, often given by Hubbard himself, and even a Roycroft Inn for guests. By the time of Janet Ashbee's visit 175 people were employed and the community was supported by the sales of the *Philistine*. Hubbard condemned socialistic communes, saying that a system must be allowed to build economically by natural expansion, and certainly his catalogues show a sound business sense.

Janet Ashbee wrote: 'Everyone here has heard of Elbert Hubbard, the Crank, the Socialist, the Bookmaker, the Heretic, the Anarkist with a K, — and most people have seen the queer stuff they turn out at the Roycroft Shop, all colours and types of paper and bindings, with now and again a successful fluke . . . The nicest part is that Fra Elbertus has a fine sense of humour, and sees the joke of the whole thing as much as anyone.'[26] The Roycroft press produced such books as Hubbard's series of *Little Journeys* — lives of great authors, painters, American statesmen and business men — or *The Book of the Roycrofters* described in the 1910 catalogue thus: 'Appreciation is an art — a fine art. Some say it is a lost art. Look into the Book of the Roycrofters: There it is, big and bold — a fine loving, living art. There you will find appreciation of a beautiful story — of the homely grace of the working-day world and its people . . . A glowing message out of the present to the people now on earth . . . Price, One Dollar.' Or, again, *The Fra Magazine,* described as 'making itself felt for its true phosphorescent qualities. It is a journal of affirmations, and says things. The early volumes will increase in value. Gather them while ye may.' Although hardly a man with the character or ideals of Morris, the Ashbees liked him and he visited them in Chipping Campden and corresponded sporadically for several years. Much of the Roycroft work which survives today is of good quality and some good design, though the plain oak furniture shows the strong influence of Gustav Stickley. Janet Ashbee commented that there was a lack of any real artistic eye within the community and that much of the design was inorganic and aesthetically poor. Hubbard and his wife drowned aboard the Lusitania in 1916, when Ashbee wrote to his wife: 'How horrible this Lusitania affair is! And your old friend Elbert Hubbard has gone down with the rest! Well, it shows that even a charlatan may be a brave man, for he went down with a brave word on his lips. "It would be glorious to die by a torpedo, and it would be a splendid advertisement"! American and characteristic.'

During his three trips in America Ashbee took great interest in the small craft communities which he was able to visit. One has the impression in his Journals, after the dissolution of his own Guild of Handicraft in 1909, that this hope for the future in the existence of other groups who had found ways to survive economically, was his primary interest. In writing of his own experiences with the Guild system and the social impossibility of its financial continuance there is occasionally the tone of near despair, as in 1903: 'Have we been

26 Janet Ashbee: C. R. Ashbee, unpublished letters and journals (King's College, Cambridge).

deluding ourselves all these years thinking we were doing any sort of good work . . . Will 2 or 3 years see us out? Is it all going to bust? . . . — Here is Liberty putting £10,000 into the Cymric Silver Co. [not in fact so] and we struggling to get our hundreds and having to potboil with vile brooches etc. to make ends meet.' It was perhaps with this voice still in his ears that he visited two communities in June 1915: Byrdcliffe, in Ulster County, New York, and the Elverhoj Colony overlooking the Hudson River near Washington.

His visit to Ralf Ratcliffe Whitehead's workshops at Byrdcliffe in fact followed its demise. Whitehead was a rich and eccentric Englishman who had first gone to California around 1895 in order to promote manual training in the schools there; however, the Santa Barbara school board remained unconvinced so he set off to establish his own Arts and Crafts colony, eventually choosing Ulster County nearby as he found that Woodstock was the only village in the Catskills that had no Jewish property owners. Despite his acknowledged debt to Morris for his ideas, his anti-Semitism may well have influenced his desire to set up his own protected community. Ashbee wrote that Whitehead had 'sought to solve the problem of the Arts and Crafts in the manner of the Grand Seigneur' but as in his own experience 'machine competition and dilettantism, as elsewhere, have done the inevitable. Whitehead is the English country gentleman transplanted into the Catskills . . . The landscape is wonderful; the conception superb; the houses, — craftsmen's houses with delightful workshops, — finely placed; there are kilns, metal shops, weaving sheds, a guest house, a central hall with library, good books and fine workmanship; the shell of a great life, and all empty but for two or three lonely spinsters, one metal worker, one weaver, and two potters. It was tragic.'[27]

At the Elverhoj Colony, run by a Dane named Anderson, there was a metal shop, tapestry room and silversmith and an etcher, R. M. Pearson, worked there. Ashbee's journal entry sums up the innate concern for the craftsman's way of life which was the main cause of his disagreement with Frank Lloyd Wright:

> The real thing is the life; and it doesn't matter so very much if their metalwork is second rate. Give them their liberty of production and they'll do it better. It's quite a simple proposition. We cannot measure the output of these personal shops by the high standards of the best. That is what we in England have been doing, — we of the Arts and Crafts, — and thus have made of a great social movement a narrow and tiresome little aristocracy working with high skill for the very rich. We have got to devise a way, — it must be done by keeping alive the personal traditions of each shop or group of shops, — to employ and keep employed the quiet, conscientious, if you like, stupid craftsman, — the man with sympathy,

35 C.R. Ashbee — Silver salt cellar set with chrysophrases and with a glass liner, 1900.

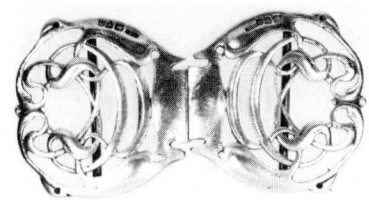

36 Liberty and Co., – 'Cymric' silver buckle, 1899.

½ Full of shit *DEGENERATE MIND*

27 Ibid.

37 Morris and Co. – 'Saville'
armchair, designed by George Jack,
c. 1890.

38

39

Opposite above
38 William De Morgan – *(left)* Rice dish, painted by Charles Passenger in 'Persian colours', W. De Morgan signature and 'CP' monogram on base; *(centre)* 'Isnik' circular dish, painted by Charles Passenger; *(right)* 'Amphora' vase painted in 'Persian' colours, all early Fulham period, 1888-97.

Opposite below
39 William De Morgan – Lustre-ware dishes, decorated in ruby lustre and ochre pigment.

ESSEX·AND·COMPANY'S

WESTMINSTER·WALL·PAPERS

114·AND·116·VICTORIA·STREET
WESTMINSTER

40 C.F.A. Voysey – Advertising material for Essex and Co., *c.* 1899.

kindliness, but no genius, who can express with his hands, — the man who wants to lead a clean life, wants humbly to invent, has no business gift but knows somehow where lies the joy of life; — in short the Democracy. England may stand for quality, but America will have the last word.

Ashbee's own views had softened since his first somewhat critical visit to the United States in 1896.

Another community which showed an equally highly individualistic interpretation of Morris' ideals was the Rose Valley Community at Moylan, near Philadelphia. It was started in 1901 by an architect, William L. Price; avowedly based on Morris' *News from Nowhere,* it also incorporated the original aspirations of Shaker furniture, stressing the moral didacticism of such productions. *News from Nowhere* had depicted life after a socialist revolution, when the place of the machine would have been established in the true craftsman perspective, abolishing the social injustices created by its power in Morris' own time. Price, however, had merely retired from industrial Philadelphia to his own community (which only survived for eight years before bankruptcy) from whence he levied invective on the system he scorned. In his magazine *The Artsman,* concluding an article on 'The Building of a chair', he summed up his philosophy:

> . . . your built chair is something more than a good chair, it is a message of honesty and joy to the possessor, and a cause of growth and joy to the worker. And your 'made-up' chair is something less than the sham that it stands for, insidiously and in the guise of a blessing undoing the character alike of maker and possessor. It and its kindred shams are the symptoms of that loosening of character that is reflected in the hideous political and industrial corruption that . . . is at work undermining our social and political fabric.[28]

The socialism of such a community is certainly suspect in as much as it can have done little practical good to anyone outside Rose Valley and it serves as an example of how the social aims of the Arts and Crafts movement could come to be dismissed as merely 'artsy-craftsy', as a subject for cranks. Although the English Guilds movement was certainly financially impractical, placing idealism above materialism, freedom of work above wages and general living standards, it was so because of a refusal to compromise those ideals which were indubitably threatened. However, there will always be a narrow margin between an unwillingness to compromise and simple eccentricity.

Gradually the idioms of Arts and Crafts design were becoming essentially middle class. As with Morris & Co., this was mainly for obvious economic reasons, but it was also because the style became a sign for a certain liberalism and education. Women were beginning to aspire to greater freedoms and the Arts and Crafts movement allowed them,

28 W. L. Price, *The Artsman*, Vol. I, No. 8, May 1904.

41

42

through magazines and in practical forms, as in art pottery, to bring some education to their homes. As the inspiration of the movement led more people to reject traditional styles and to evolve their own decorative schemes, its impetus gave way to design which was emphatically removed from a simple working man's home. Designers took freedom of expression to a peak and produced fine, even palatial decorative schemes, such as the work of L. C. Tiffany or Baillie-Scott's Darmstadt interiors. The designs of Voysey, Webb or Stickley still held to the expression of explicit social aims through a specific vernacular which referred back to the original ideals of the movement; in the honesty of construction, lack of applied ornament and stress on the nature of the material employed was a vocabulary of the social position of the craftsman. However, the work of Mackintosh and the Glasgow School in Britain and of Frank Lloyd Wright and his successors in America showed the beginnings of an elegance in home life for its own sake, no longer specifically tied to such educational or social aims. It is this emancipated middle class ethic which found its way to the West Coast of America as Arts and Crafts.

A fine example of the sensibility which welcomed Arts and Crafts on the West Coast is given by Robert W. Winter in *California Design — 1910*, in his description of Charles Fletcher Lummis, editor of the Los Angeles *Times*:

He was a man of culture who affected a corduroy suit. He was a champion of the civil rights of all Indians, but when

41 C.R. Ashbee – Electric ceiling light from Ashbee's house, 'The Magpie and Stump', *c.* 1895.

42 C.R. Mackintosh – Electric ceiling light from the Room-de-Luxe in the Willow tea-rooms, Glasgow, 1904.

it came to collecting elements of their culture, he usually chose the New Mexico variety, that is, the ones who made magnificent pottery (which he collected as Easteners collect Greek pots or Chinese bronzes), danced through gorgeous ceremonials (which he photographed), and sang songs which he could adapt to the chromatic scale of his civilisation and record in his own voice on records . . . In other words he chose a culture which, though exotic, was at the same time easily accessible to someone educated in the traditional values of Harvard.[29]

Robert Winter is talking of the culture of the Arroyo, Pasadena, the orange-groves where nature and culture could keep company. California was the 'West of the West', the Pacific coast the final frontier to the pioneers who followed the gold rush to San Francisco and opportunity down to Los Angeles, which had begun to be settled around the 1880s. Despite being a land of immigration with mixed cultures, the Arts and Crafts spirit took hold — or, rather, the Craftsman spirit, for California learnt more from the East and Midwest than from Europe.

In 1909 George Wharton James, who had been an associate editor on Stickley's *Craftsman,* published the one and only issue of the *Arroyo Craftsman.* The magazine was linked to the Arroyo Guild, a group of men and women 'ready to do anything' among the various craft skills, from stained glass to carpets. By 1915 the Guild had disappeared but it is interesting that in such a new culture the spirit of reform, which coming from England brought with it the necessary implications of a revival, could catch the imagination of what was perhaps the intellectual élite. The revival which was entailed in and around Pasadena was that of C. F. Lummis, that of the Spanish-Mexican past and of the American Indians. As A. F. Mathews, the Director of the California School of Design, wrote: 'All artists are influenced. A school in the true sense is a series of counter influences — a system of active and reactive forces which brings forward a central or dominant quality.'[30] What is brought out in the architecture of southern California are many different influences, from Swiss chalets, to Mission forms, to Japanese styles. What is brought out in the espousal of Arts and Crafts is an inherent romanticism in a return to a lost or disappearing past, the joy of nostalgia.

Charles and Henry Greene were perhaps the most successful architects of this period. Their early work (from 1893) shows an adherence to conservative styles, but from 1903-9 they worked within the Arts and Crafts idiom, designing their own decorative schemes and successfully adapting Japanese influences. C. R. Ashbee met Charles Sumner Greene in Pasadena in 1909 and wrote in his Journal:

He fetched us in his auto this afternoon and drove us about. They took us to his workshops where they were making without exception the best and most characteristic furniture I have seen in this country. There were

29 Robert W. Winter, *California Design 1910*, Ed. Andersen, Moore and Winter, p. 14, California Design Publications 1974.

30 A. F. Mathews, quoted in *Mathews: Masterpieces of the California Decorative Style*, p. 44, The Oakland Museum, 1972.

43

44

beautiful cabinets and chairs of walnut and lignum vitae, exquisite dowelling and pegging, and in all a supreme feeling for the material, quite up to our best English craftsmanship . . . I have not felt so at home in any workshop on this side of the Atlantic . . . I noticed — 'tis the old story — that the men who were doing the work were old men and some quite old. I talked with one of them — men who had still a traditional feeling for Craftmanship in woods, and who had learned their trade before the days of machine development and before the American wood crafts had become 'grand-rapidized'.[31]

The Greenes continued working until 1923, but after 1909 they lost much of the Craftsman simplicity. It is said that when asked why his architecture was so good, Charles Greene replied, 'Why, I think it was because we had rich clients.'[32] However, as Ashbee implicitly said, the excellence of craftsmanship, at least to his English understanding, lay in the skill of the craftsmen and the elements he most admired could not be achieved merely through financial possibility — Ashbee's concern still lay with the worker and the spirit he could instil in an item of furniture and less with the excellence of production, especially if machines were introduced to do the work. That aspect of the original aims of the Victorian Arts and Crafts movement had been lost in the passage of time and place.

In San Francisco, after the earthquakes and fire of 1906, there was a great awareness of the opportunity given to re-build the city in the best way. Such views are consistently put forward in A. F. Mathews' *Philopolis*, which was as much

43 Charles Sumner Greene – Detail of a teak mirror, hung by leather straps, made for the Blacker house, 1909.

44 Peter Waals – Detail of an oval, oak, gate-leg dining-table showing chamfering and pegged joints, *c*. 1930.

45 William De Morgan – Tile decorated with two rabbits in ruby lustre, *c*. 1890.

46 William De Morgan – Tile decorated with a leaping ibex in ruby lustre, *c*. 1890.

47 Ernest A. Batchelder – Cast ceramic tile, *c*. 1909.

48 Ernest A. Batchelder – Cast ceramic tile, *c*. 1909.

31 N.B. 'Grand-rapidized' is a reference to Gustav Stickley's workshops at Grand Rapids.

32 *California Design 1910*, ibid. p. 28. C. S. Greene cited.

45

46

47

48

concerned with fine civic engineering as with art. Mathews and his wife Lucia opened 'The Furniture Shop' through which they executed large interior schemes and single pieces of furniture, with carved and brightly painted ornament by Lucia herself. Both painters, they included in their work the qualities of light and colour of California as well as the local flora, although Arthur Mathews' work betrays the classicism of his Paris training. In many ways their murals and interior schemes are like the later work of the Omega Workshops in London, although the differences in climate are all too apparent. Although no more explicitly attached to the Arts and Crafts movement than were Roger Fry, Duncan Grant and Vanessa Bell in the Omega, the Mathews' work represents a high point in the quality which the movement strove towards. And it was well that the essential qualities of a movement which began in England to fight for freedom amid oppression should appear in the 'land of opportunity'.

By the end of the 19th century much had been done to educate the public as a whole in matters of aesthetic taste. *The Studio* had done much towards propagating ideas, both through the extensive coverage of their articles and through their design competitions, and Liberty & Co. in London, Samuel Bing's 'Galeries de l'Art Nouveau' in Paris and L. C. Tiffany in New York were established fountainheads for the new design. The Guild movement had done much to bring such ideas closer to working people all over England, such as the Keswick School of Industrial Art founded in 1884 or the Northern Art-Workers' Guild with which Walter Crane was involved. Other guilds were the wood-carving class organised by the Princess of Wales (later Queen Alexandra) at Sandringham, the Duchess of Sutherland's Cripples' Guild, Mabel de Grey's classes at Pimlico and Walsingham, Norfolk, the 'Clarion' Guild, formed for the benefit of the employees of that paper in Leeds, and Mr. and Mrs. Godfrey Blount's embroidery Guild in Haslemere. In 1884 the Home Arts and Industries Association had been established, dedicated to the revival of village crafts, and the exhibitions held at the Albert Hall provided an admirable shop-window for the products of these local guilds. However, although the Arts and Crafts was a movement dedicated to secular and democratic design, the problem still existed of reconciling that art to the machine. Although the educated architect-craftsman now worked alongside his workmen, it was a tiny minority of working people who felt the impact of Morris's social aims. Except perhaps in the textile and wallpaper trades, most manufacturers resisted the aims of the movement and the worker remained divorced from any true creative enterprise. Well into the twentieth century English decorative styles remained rooted in the Arts and Crafts movement and attempts to absorb a more theoretical, industrial ethic of design were all but ignored.

By the beginning of the twentieth century F. L. Wright's statement of 1901 that 'the tall modern office building is the

49

machine pure and simple . . . the engine, the motor, and the battle-ship (are) the works of art of the century!'[33] was being recognized and his work was pointing the way forward from architecture in America. In Britain, although the work of C. R. Mackintosh and the Glasgow School can be seen retrospectively to have bridged the gap between the eclectic architectural styles of Philip Webb and his associates and the beginnings of new styles which were totally independent of past traditions, their work was largely ignored in England. It was acclaimed abroad, especially by Josef Hoffman in Vienna, where the machine was beginning to be recognized as having a place in the world of art.

49 Richard Norman Shaw – Detail of an oak bookcase, 1861.

33 Frank Lloyd Wright, 'The Art and Craft of the Machine', a paper read at Hull House, 1901. Quoted in H. Allen Brooks' *The Prairie School*, University of Toronto Press, 1972, p. 20.

50 Ernest Gimson – Detail of handles made by Alfred Bucknell from a walnut and ebony sideboard, *c.* 1910.

50

It has been said that the Arts and Crafts movement was instrumental in changes both aesthetic and social. Its real aims were to educate people to an awareness that craft and the craftsman were worthy of protection and despite the leaps forward in design at the beginning of this century, these ideals were still maintained. Where James Nasmyth, the inventor of the steam hammer, and himself a major employer, had noted in the nineteenth century that one effect of strikes (Unions had been legalized in 1824) was a large increase in the use of self-acting machines which would make redundant the better organised, skilled craftsman, and free the owners from the power of organised labour,[34] in the twentieth century the craftsman was to become embattled because of the indifference of the public to his trade. In 1934 in *Art and Industry* Herbert Read wrote of Morris and his legacy of design for machine-made products, that he 'was a good influence, but essentially a superficial one. It was mainly in the sphere of applied ornament and decoration, and did not touch the more fundamental problems of form.' Problems which were by 1934 defined in relation to the machine: however, 'Morris's attitude is complicated by ethical considerations which most of us find sympathetic.' In 1929 Sir George Trevelyan went to work in Peter Waals's workshops for two years and later wrote of the discipline to be found in such a way of life, of 'the accumulated skill of a lifetime, secreted in fingers and brain and infallible judgement of eye, nowhere recorded, built through the group experience of a craft team over a generation . . .'[35] This experience is one which most people will find sympathetic, but which few will now know: it is the experience which men such as Ashbee and Morris were fighting to preserve.

'The Gimson-Barnsley-Waals tradition drew on a native

34 James Nasmyth, *An Autobiography*, ed. Samuel Smiles, 1885, 3rd edition, p. 311.

35 36 Sir George Trevelyan, Bt. *The Workshop of Peter Waals: A Tribute from a pupil*, exhibition catalogue, 'Ernest Gimson', Leicester Museum, 1969.

51 Sidney Barnsley – Detail of walnut wardrobe with metalwork by Ernest Gimson. Commissioned for Lady Waterlow, c. 1905.

English genius going back through centuries of handling timber in the building of ships and houses and great tythe-barns. Thus as *woodwork* this tradition stands unrivalled in its honesty and unsentimentality . . . It contained as Waals expressed in a late letter, a quality of "truth".'[36] In 1890 inspired by the same ideals as the original Morris, Marshall, Faulkner & Co., Ernest Gimson, Sidney Barnsley, W. R. Lethaby, Mervyn McCartney and Reginald Blomfield formed Kenton and Company, employing four or five professional cabinet makers with a capital of £600. The company was dissolved in 1892 for financial reasons, but the men involved had gained invaluable experience in furniture design and workshop conditions. In 1893 Gimson and the Barnsleys moved to Ewen near Cirencester, and the following year to a workshop at Pinbury Park, settling permanently at Sapperton in 1903 in cottages of their own design. In 1901 they had been joined by a Dutch cabinet maker, Peter Waals, who continued to work, using some of Gimson's designs, until his death in 1937. Sidney Barnsley described his way of life at Sapperton in a letter to Philip Webb thus:

> My Workshop which I have to my 'lone self' is a great improvement upon the Pinbury one, much better lighted

36 Ibid.

52 Peter Waals – Detail of oak handles from the double panelled doors of a gentleman's wardrobe, *c.* 1934.

and being thatched is warmer and drier, and from the end window I have a most wonderful view of across the valley to the hanging wood you would remember. I am still occupied principally in making good solid oak furniture with occasional pieces of a more delicate kind as a rest and change. I have just finished two tables of English oak, 12′ 0″ by 3′ 6″ each, the tops out of 3″ and with only one joint in the width and they have given me a fair dressing down and by night time I have felt fairly tired out . . . Last week I heard of an old table in Glamorganshire 41′ 8½″ by 2′ 9″ by 6″ in one piece!![37]

As Ashbee wrote in 1911, '. . . that theoretical socialism and labour politics have always taken a second place in the mind of the workman whenever his work was intrinsically interesting',[38] so the descriptions of the working conditions at Sapperton and the preoccupations of the craftsmen seldom include the political issues so alive to Ashbee himself and his contemporaries. The Cotswold designers were seldom short of work, although it is interesting to note that from 1901-1919 Peter Waals' wages rose from £2 10s. 0d. to £5 0s. 0d.!

It is perhaps more important in writing of craftsmen to describe their work process and problems, rather than

37 Letter from Sidney Barnsley to Philip Webb, Sapperton, on Cirencester, 1 May 1904, Cheltenham Museum.

38 C. R. Ashbee, *Should We Stop Teaching Art?*, 1911.

historical details, for this is what is truly Arts and Crafts. Obviously, what the Cotswold designers least wrote about was their day-to-day activities and the constant atmosphere of the life they lived. All that can be done is to give examples such as the foregoing, or such as this letter from Edward Gardiner, who worked for them, to Sidney Barnsley's son Edward, who is himself a furniture maker:

> Here is a story told me by Alfred Bucknell [the local blacksmith who carried out Gimson's designs] of how when he came upon a problem he went to bed and stayed there till he had solved it. I tried the plan, on my rush and other problems, and it worked out. The difference between Bucknell and myself was that when he got stuck he went straight to bed and got on with the thinking as part of his days work whereas I waited until night came and it was bedtime. Lying there quietly and using the darkness as a blackboard I could visualise the processes in my mind and keep trying them out mentally until I had one that seemed workable. In the morning I would try it out and find it worked.
>
> Later on I re-rushed old chairs and carefully unravelling the old work I found I had discovered the right way. Incidentally by looking through old rush seats one can very often pick up some useful methods that have been hidden for years.[39]

The productions of the Cotswold school are examples of a lifetime of woodwork and, perhaps especially in Ernest

53 Ernest Gimson's workshop at Pinbury Mill, which he shared for some time with Sidney and Ernest Barnsley, photo c. 1894.

39 *Edward Gardiner's Story*, a letter from Edward Gardiner to Edward Barnsley, 1956. Quoted in full in the exhibition catalogue 'Ernest Gimson', Leicestershire Museum 1969.

54 Guild of Handicraft – The metalwork shop at Essex House, photo before 1902.

Gimson's case, of the Arts and Crafts way of life. Gimson, an architect, never made any furniture with his own hands, except some turned ash chairs with rush seats made during his short apprenticeship at Ledbury, and yet he had a fine and distinctive understanding of his materials and processes and was constantly refining his working plans. He did not despise the machine, but held to W. R. Lethaby's belief that a machine-made object could only ever be second best to one made by hand. Gimson was a strict overseer, but held it important that his men derived satisfaction from their work. Most of the men who worked at Sapperton set up their own workshops after Gimson's death in 1919 and the spirit of their craftsmanship was continued in Broadway by Gordon Russell.

In 1915 however, the initial impetus of the Arts and Crafts movement, indeed of the 1836 Government Reports and official involvement in the 1851 Exhibition, led to the setting up of the Design and Industries Association. This organisation was to promote co-operation between workers, designers, manufacturers, distributors, educators and the general public,

55

56 C.R. Ashbee – Door-handle from 'The Magpie and Stump', Ashbee's house in Chelsea, 1895.

57 Frank Brangwyn – Silver-plated cupboard handle, c. 1910.

and to promote the best of British design through exhibitions. Its work was made more urgent by the economic changes of the war years. That the DIA from the first accepted the necessity of the machine as an essential component in modern design was ratified in 1920 with the formation, by the Boards of Trade and Education, of the British Institute of Industrial Art which co-operated with the DIA and the Civic Arts Association. As design and art teaching were progressively officially organised (with the help and involvement of many of the leading Arts and Crafts designers) the movement as a coherent unity was gradually dissolved. Other experiments in personal art, such as the short-lived but admirable Omega Workshops, did exist, but no longer under the aegis of the nineteenth century movement. Fine craftsmanship reverted to established and financially secure organisations, such as Heal's — perhaps the most famous store for good design. None of this, however, would have been possible without the fervour of the Arts and Crafts movement, although in the end that fervour had to be content with official compromise. To look back now, the deepest aspirations of the movement are still to be attained.

> What I seek to show is that this Arts and Crafts movement . . . is not what the public has thought it to be, or is seeking to make it: a nursery for luxuries, a hothouse for the production of mere trivialities and useless things for the rich . . . To the men of this movement, who are seeking to compass the destruction of the commercial system, to discredit it, undermine it, overthrow it, their mission is just as serious and just as sacred as was that of their great grandfathers who first helped raise it into being, and thought that they had built for it an abiding monument in a crystal palace of glass and iron.

C. R. Ashbee *Craftsmanship in Competitive Industry*, 1908.

55 Guild of Handicraft – The blacksmith's shop.

CHRONOLOGY

1819   Birth of John Ruskin

1834   Birth of William Morris

1848   'Pre-Raphaelite Brotherhood' formed and first Pre-Raphaelite works exhibited.

1849   Paris: 11th Trade Exhibition. Visited by Henry Cole, and Matthew Digby Wyatt, who had been asked to prepare a report on the Exhibition for the Society of Arts. It was this exhibition which was the inspiration for the Great Exhibition organised by Henry Cole and Prince Albert.

1851   London: The 'Great Exhibition' (the Great Exhibition of the Works of Industry of All Nations), held under the direction of the Prince Consort and Sir Henry Cole. Allegedly visited by Morris, then aged 17, who was nauseated by the tasteless and materialistic display.

1853   Great Industrial Exhibition, Dublin.
World's Fair of the Works of Industry of all Nations, New York.

1854   Working Men's College started in London by F. D. Maurice.

1855   Paris: L'Exposition Universelle des Produits de l'Industrie de toutes les Nations, included the works of the Pre-Raphaelites which had a considerable influence on the French Realist School.

1856   Owen Jones' *The Grammar of Ornament* published, the first book to have full-colour plates printed by chromolithography.

1857   American Institute of Architects founded in New York.
October: An exhibition of British Painting opened in New York, going on to Washington, Philadelphia and Boston, including Pre-Raphaelite works assembled by Ernest Gambart. The show was not a success due to the current decline in the U.S. economy.
Rossetti undertook the decoration of the Oxford Union library with the assistance of William Morris and other members of the Pre-Raphaelite circle.

1859   Planning and building of Morris' Red House by Philip Webb at Upton in Kent. Furniture designed, especially made and decorated for the house by Morris, Webb, Rossetti and Burne-Jones. The interior was decorated with fresco painting.

1861   Morris, Marshall, Faulkner & Co. founded to provide the type of furniture so conspicuously lacking in the mid nineteenth century — solidly constructed and without superfluous ornament. Madox Brown, Rossetti and Burne-Jones all worked for the firm, as did Arthur Hughes, another Pre-Raphaelite, albeit briefly. The foreman glass-worker was George Campfield, a recruit from the Working Men's College.

1862   London: International Exhibition. Included a stand furnished by Morris & Co. which was praised for archaeological exactness of their imitation of the style of the Middle Ages, and the first Japanese art and craft works to be widely seen, which had an immediate and widespread effect on the design of the period.

1866   Morris & Co. undertook two important commissions; the decoration of the Green Dining Room at the South Kensington Museum and of the Armoury and Tapestry Room at St. James's Palace.

1867   Paris: L'Exposition Universelle.

1871   1st South Kensington Exhibition.
Ruskin's *Fors Clavigera* began to appear in instalments and was eagerly read by A. H. Mackmurdo, amongst others.

1872   2nd South Kensington Exhibition.
William De Morgan, who had been working since the early days of the firm for Morris & Co., set up his own pottery in Chelsea.

1873   'Martin Brothers' pottery established by the brothers Robert, Wallace, Edwin and Charles Martin in Fulham.
Vienna: Universal Exhibition.
3rd South Kensington Exhibition.

1874   Morris began his experiments with fabric design.
4th South Kensington Exhibition.

1875   Formation of 'Liberty & Co.', a shop specialising in Oriental art and artefacts. Patrons of the new shop included E. W. Godwin, D. G. Rossetti, Burne-Jones and Whistler. Christopher Dresser, after his visit to Japan, also attempted to open a business selling Oriental goods (Dresser and Holme set up in 1878 in Farringdon Road) and in 1880 was appointed Art Manager of the Art Furnishers' Alliance. Both businesses failed. Dresser's son Louis, however, later worked for Liberty & Co.
Jonathan T. Carr began the building of Bedford Park, Chiswick, employing E. W. Godwin and Norman Shaw as architects. Completed in 1881, it was an attempt to create a colony of artistic interiors. W. B. Yeats was among the first to live there.

1876   Philadelphia: Centennial Exposition. The displays of both Oriental pottery and E. Chaplet's 'Limoges' glazes influenced studio potters in America, especially Hugh C. Robertson and M. Louise McLaughlin. Christopher Dresser lectured in Philadelphia that year and his influence can be clearly seen in the change of style of Daniel Pabst's work, which had been exhibited that year. Dresser was also commissioned to make a collection of Japanese artefacts, including glass, for Tiffany & Co. while he was in Japan in 1877.

1877   M. Louise McLaughlin developed 'Limoges' underglaze painting.
New York Society of Decorative Art founded 24th February.
Martin Bros. moved from Fulham to Southall.
Morris founded 'Anti-Scrape', the 'Society for the Protection of Ancient Buildings'.

1878   Herter Bros. of New York designed the interior of the Mark Hopkins House, San Francisco, to which the California School of Design moved in 1893.
Paris: L'Exposition Universelle.
London: International Exhibition at South Kensington.

1879 C. H. Brannam Ltd. established in Barnstable, Devon by Charles Brannam for the production of art pottery, known as 'Barum Ware', which was featured later in Liberty & Co. catalogues.
Louis C. Tiffany & Co., Associated Artists, founded in New York with the co-operation of Candace Wheeler and the Society of Decorative Art.
Women's Pottery Club founded in Cincinnati to provide useful and artistic means of gaining an income for women.
London: International Exhibition at South Kensington.

1880 Rookwood Pottery founded in Cincinnati.

1881 Fourth American edition of Eastlake's *Hints on Household Taste* published. It was first serialised in *Queen*, 1865–6 and proved incredibly successful in America, giving rise to the 'Eastlake style'.
Aller Vale Pottery reorganised for the production of Art Pottery after a fire had destroyed the old factory which specialised in architectural wares. Later stocked by Liberty & Co.

1882 Partnership of Henry Tooth and William Ault established by the Bretby Art Pottery.
Messrs Wilcox of Leeds began the manufacture of Burmantofts Faience which continued until 1904.
Oscar Wilde, undertook a wildly successful eighteen months lecture tour of America, preaching the Aesthetic ideal of art and decoration.
Century Guild founded by A. H. Mackmurdo, Selwyn Image and Herbert P. Horne.
The architect H. H. Richardson travelled to Europe and visited Morris at Merton Abbey and here he met Burne-Jones and showed 'unbounded enthusiasm' for De Morgan's work.

1882/3 L. C. Tiffany & Co., Associated Artists, decorated the White House.

1883 Mackmurdo's book on *Wren's City Churches* published with the famous title page, now seen as a seminal influence on Art Nouveau.
The Ladies Home Journal founded in America: it was later to contain articles on Arts and Crafts design.
Boston, U.S.A., The American Exhibition of the Products, Arts and Manufactures of Foreign Nations.

1884 First appearance of *The Hobby Horse*, a quarterly magazine of the Century Guild. Printed on hand-made paper with the advice and assistance of Emery Walker it is a precursor of Morris' experiments with fine printing at the Kelmscott Press.
Art Worker's Guild formed by the pupils and assistants of Richard Norman Shaw joining together with the 'Fifteen', a group launched some four years earlier on the initiative of Lewis F. Day.
Keswick School of Industrial Art founded as an evening institute by Canon and Mrs Rawnsley.

1885 Home Arts and Industries Association established by Mrs Jebb with the enthusiastic support of A. H. Mackmurdo.
The annual exhibitions held at the Royal Albert Hall show work of all the local classes and guilds.

1886 Liverpool Exhibition. Mackmurdo's stand provided yet more easily assimilated inspiration for the Art Nouveau artists of the *fin de siècle*. The elongated roof-supports ending in wide flat ornamental finials are the prototypes of many later architectural decorative features.

1886/7   C. R. Ashbee went to live at Toynbee Hall, the pioneer University Settlement in the East End of London. He lectured at places such as Deptford or Beckton, 'of Gas Works fame' to recruit men for Toynbee Hall. There he started a Ruskin reading class which he expanded into a class of drawing and decoration. He supervised the decoration of the Toynbee Hall dining room by the members of his class, and it was from these pupils that the nucleus of his Guild of Handicraft was drawn.

1888   Guild of Handicraft founded with three members and a working capital of fifty pounds. Despite Morris' doubts — he met Ashbee's plans 'with a great deal of cold water' — the Guild was remarkably successful for many years, only running into financial difficulties in 1907.
Art and Crafts Exhibition Society founded by splinter group from the Art Workers' Guild. The founder members included Walter Crane, Heywood Sumner, W. A. S. Benson, William De Morgan, Lewis F. Day and W. R. Lethaby. It was another of their number, T. Cobden Sanderson who coined the felicitous phrase Arts and Crafts to replace the clumsy title originally used of 'The Combined Arts Society'. The first exhibition was held at the New Gallery in October.
National Association for the Advancement of Art in Relation to Industry formed. At both the first Congress in Liverpool, and at Edinburgh the following year, Morris and Crane spoke on socialist issues and were said to have 'spoiled the Congress (!)'.
Glasgow International Exhibition.

1889   Paris: Exposition Universelle Internationale.
An exhibition of American work was held at Johnstone, Norman & Co. Galleries in New Bond Street; it included decorative designs by John la Farge and Rookwood faience.

1890   Establishment of the Kelmscott Press, the venture that was to dominate Morris' last years.
Birmingham Guild of Handicraft founded with Montague Fordham as first director.
Vittoria Street School for jewellers and silversmiths opened in Birmingham.
Kenton and Co., the furniture firm, founded by Ernest Gimson, Sidney Barnsley, Alfred Powell, Mervyn Macartney, W. R. Lethaby and Reginald Blomfield.
Charles Rohlfs opened his furniture workshop in Buffalo.
Walter Crane visited America.
The work of C. F. A. Voysey first began appearing in American journals.

1891   Kenton & Co. exhibition at Barnard's Inn, the premises of the Art Workers' Guild. In spite of the success of the exhibition the Company failed in 1892.
Arts and Crafts exhibition held in Brussels, inspired the foundation of *L'Association Pour L'Art*.
Chelsea Pottery opened in Chelsea, Mass. by Hugh C. Robertson.
George and Albert Stickley established Stickley Bros. Co. in Grand Rapids.
Voysey's work was exhibited at the Boston Architectural Club.

1892   Walter Crane lectured at the Art Institute of Chicago.
Elbert Hubbard, the founder of the Roycrofters, visited Morris at Hammersmith and saw the Kelmscott Press which was to inspire his own experiments in fine printing.

1893   Chicago: World's Columbian Exposition; World's Fair. Included exhibits by Tiffany & Co. and demonstrated the great advance in American artistic culture since 1876.
The first number of *The Studio* was published in April, including an interview with C. F. A. Voysey, articles on Morris' decoration at Stanmore Hall, the work by students at Birmingham Town Hall, and work by Walter Crane, A. H. Mackmurdo and Frank

Brangwyn. It was this propagandist magazine which disseminated the activities and ideals of the Arts and Crafts movement.

Frank Lloyd Wright set up his own architectural practise in Chicago.

Voysey's work first appeared in the *International Studio* and was also exhibited at the Chicago World's Fair.

1894   Della Robbia pottery established by Harold Rathbone in Birkenhead.
Grueby Faience Co. started in Boston.

1895   Samuel Bing published his *La Culture Artistique en Amerique*, the result of his observations made during a trip to the United States in 1893 to visit the Chicago World's Fair. At the end of the same year he altered his shop, which had previously concentrated on the sale of objects imported from the Far East, into a showcase for modern designers and craftsmen; now known as the *Galeries de l'Art Nouveau*.
Birmingham Guild of Handicraft became a Limited Company with the Right Hon. William Kenrick M.P. as a director.
Newcomb College pottery established in New Orleans for women students.
Chalk and Chisel Club organised in Minneapolis, which later became the Minneapolis Arts and Crafts Society in 1899.
Venice: Esposizione Internazionale d'Arte (1st Biennale).
Liège: L'Œuvres Artistiques exhibition.

1896   Death of William Morris in October.
Foundation of the Central School of Arts and Crafts with W. R. Lethaby and George Frampton as joint principals, in November.
C. R. Mackintosh won the competition to provide the design for the new Glasgow School of Art.
The Song of Songs completed at Roycroft by Elbert Hubbard.
C. R. Ashbee visited New York and Philadelphia.
Dedham Pottery opened in Dedham, Massachusetts with Hugh C. Robertson as director after the failure of the Chelsea Pottery.
First issue of *House Beautiful* published in Chicago.

1897   Pilkington's, the glass manufacturers, established their pottery, manufacturing tiles and other wares designed by Walter Crane, Lewis F. Day and C. F. A. Voysey.
First major Arts and Crafts exhibition held at Copley Hall, Boston in April. On June 28th the Boston Arts and Crafts Society was founded.
Chicago Arts and Crafts Society founded 22nd October.
C. R. Mackintosh first undertakes the designing, decorating and furnishing of a number of tea-rooms in Glasgow for the Misses Cranston. The tea-room movement had begun in the 1870s to combat day-time drunkenness by providing billiard rooms, smoking rooms etc. Mackintosh collaborated on the Buchanan Street and Argyle Street rooms with George Walton but had complete control over the Ingram Street (1901) and Willow (1903–4) tea-rooms. The work was not completed until 1916.
Brussels: International Exhibition.
The first article on F. L. Wright appeared in *House Beautiful*. A second followed in 1899.

1898   The artists' colony at Darmstadt set up by the Grand Duke of Hesse. Furniture designs commissioned from M. H. Baillie Scott and C. R. Ashbee and made by the Guild of Handicraft.
The Ruskin Pottery established by W. Howson Taylor, son of the remarkable headmaster of the Birmingham School of Art, E. R. Taylor, who provided some of the decorative designs for the pottery. W. H. Taylor was throughout his career preoccupied

with the use of experimental glazes and the interest of Ruskin pottery lies solely in the use of glaze effects.

Omar Ramsden and Alwyn Carr set up in partnership in London establishing a recognisable style of elaborated 'Arts and Crafts' inspiration. Much of the work was carried out by assistants.

Gustave Stickley Co. founded in Syracuse, New York, in May. That year he also visited Europe, meeting Voysey, Ashbee, Samuel Bing and others.

William H. Grueby introduced matt glazes at his pottery, influencing many of the American studio potters.

Vienna: 1st Secession Exhibition. Walter Crane exhibited.

1898/9   Liberty's 'Cymric' silver range established. Many Arts and Crafts artists employed as designers, among them Arthur Gaskin, Bernard Cuzner and Reginald (Rex) Silver, but the most prolific and consistently used was the Manxman, Archibald Knox.

1899   Adelaide Alsop Robineau, an associate of the University City Pottery, Missouri, began publication of *Keramic Studio* in Syracuse, to provide good designs for other potters.

Industrial Art League founded in Chicago; disbanded in 1904.

Vienna: 3rd Secession exhibition. Walter Crane exhibited.

Venice: Esposizione Internazionale d'Arte (3rd Biennale, twenty Glasgow School exhibits).

1900   Paris: L'Exposition Universelle. This exhibition provided an unrivalled showcase for the work of Art Nouveau designers. The work of the obscure Bromsgrove Guild, founded in the early 1890s by Walter Gilbert, a cousin of the sculptor Alfred Gilbert, was by some organisational oversight, practically the only English craftwork to be seen.

In the same year both John Ruskin and Oscar Wilde died, one mad, the other disgraced.

L. and J. G. Stickley form their own company in Fayetteville, New York.

Guild of Arts and Crafts of New York organised.

C. R. Ashbee on a lecture tour of America; he met Frank Lloyd Wright at Hull House, Chicago.

Paris: Centennial exhibition.

Vienna: 8th Secession Exhibition. It included rooms by the Glasgow School and Ashbee's Guild of Handicraft.

1901   Ernest Gimson established his furniture workshops temporarily in Cirencester, where he was joined by Peter Waals, an experienced Dutch cabinet-maker.

Artificers' Guild founded by Nelson Dawson.

Buffalo: Pan-American Exposition.

Artus Van Briggle started his own pottery studio in Colorado Springs.

Rose Valley Association incorporated at Moylan, Pennsylvania by W. L. Price and M. Hawley McLanahan based on the ideals of Morris' *News from Nowhere* which had been published in England in *The Commonweal*, 1890.

The Craftsman, first published by Gustav Stickley at Syracuse in October. It contained designs for furniture and decorative schemes and was widely read in America.

Furniture Shop started by the Roycrofters at East Aurora.

Glasgow: International Exhibition.

Venice: Esposizione Internazionale d'Arte.

1902   *Handicraft*, first published in Boston.

Handicraft Guild founded in Minneapolis.

Society of Arts and Crafts founded in Grand Rapids.

Gimson's permanent workshop opened at Daneway House, Sapperton, which formed a focal point for the activities of the Cotswold School. The same year the Guild of

Handicraft moved to Chipping Campden in the same neighbourhood as Sapperton.
J. Paul Cooper appointed head of the metalwork department at the Birmingham School of Art.
Van de Velde opened a craft school in Weimar, the first of the activities leading eventually to the Bauhaus.
Tobey Furniture Co. of Chicago held an exhibition of Morris fabrics, reviewed in *House Beautiful* by an Englishman, Joseph Twyman. Marshall Field & Co. of Chicago also stocked Morris & Co. goods.
Vienna: 15th Secession exhibition. It included jewellery by Ashbee and Edgar Simpson.
Turin: Esposizione Internazionale delle Industrie e del Lavoro.

1903   William Morris Society founded in Chicago, 7th May, by Joseph Twyman.
Rose Valley Association began publication of *The Artsman*.
Henry Wilson published *Silverwork and Jewellery*.
Artificers' Guild acquired by Montague Fordham, one-time director of the Birmingham Guild of Handicraft, and re-established in his gallery in Maddox Street in London.
Vienna: 17th Secession exhibition. It included jewellery and silverwork by Ashbee.

1904   Alexander Fisher set up a school of enamelling in his Kensington studio.
St. Louis: Louisiana Purchase International Exposition, The Art Palace.
Voysey was commissioned to design a courtyard house in Massachusetts.

1905   Tiffany pottery first sold to the public.
Buffalo: Pan-American Exposition.
Liège: Exposition Universelle et Internationale.
Ernest Batchelder visited England and went to Chipping Campden where he noted a 'spirit of discontent' among the Guild members. He wrote an article on his visit, published in *The Craftsman*, 1908.
6th Biennale in Venice, the English section designed by Frank Brangwyn.

1906   C. L. Eastlake died.
California earthquake and fire.
The Furniture Shop and Philopolis Press founded in San Francisco by A. F. and L. K. Mathews. The publications of the press, including *Philipolis*, were dedicated to planning the re-building of San Francisco.
Della Robbia pottery closed.
Vienna: 24th Secession exhibition. It included silver and jewellery by Ashbee.

1907   Founding of the Deutsche Werkbund by Hermann Muthesius who had been sent in 1896 by the Prussian Board of Trade to England to make a study of English architecture and decoration.
National League of Handicraft Societies organised in Boston in February.
Last issue of *The Artsman*.
Greene & Greene begin work on the Blacker House in Pasadena.

1908   Ashbee visited America to lecture. After his visit he contributed articles to *House Beautiful*.
Dirk Van Erp opens the Copper Shop in Oakland.
Saragossa: L'Exposicio Hispanico-Francesca.

1909   Guild of Handicraft disbanded.
Modern English Silverwork, an essay by C. R. Ashbee, printed at his Essex House Press.
Only issue of the *Arroyo Craftsman* published in Los Angeles in October.
Rose Valley Community bankrupt.
Frank Lloyd Wright undertook his first West Coast commission.

Ashbee visited California and met the Greenes, comparing their adaptation of Japanese architectural features favourably with the work of Frank Lloyd Wright.

1910 Fulper Pottery Co., New Jersey began production of art pottery.
Frank Lloyd Wright's *Ausgefuehrte Bauten und Entwuerfe* published in Berlin with a foreword by Ashbee. That year he stayed with Ashbee in Chipping Campden.
Stickley was forced to admit in *The Craftsman* that not only had he never built the Craftsman Houses, which he had designed and published, but that he knew that their cost would be much higher than his estimates. *The Craftsman's* circulation began to drop from what had been its peak.
Brussels: Exposition Universelle et Internationale.

1911 Turin: International exhibition. University City pottery won the Grand Prize of Europe for Mrs. Robineau's 'scarab' vase.
In August 1911 and November 1912 articles on and by Voysey appeared in *The Craftsman*.

1912 Archibald Knox visited Philadelphia and New York.
Imprint founded by Gerald Meynell, with Edward Johnston, Ernest Jackson and J. H. Mason as editors. W. R. Lethaby contributed to it. This magazine only survived for a year, but demonstrated Britain's lead in printing and typography, following on from the Kelmscott Press.

1913 Omega Workshops opened in Fitzroy Square by Roger Fry with work by Duncan Grant, Vanessa Bell, Wyndham Lewis, Frederick Etchells and Cuthbert Hamilton. They specialised in interior decoration with murals, painted furniture, pottery and rugs. The venture, influenced by Poiret's Paris workshops, survived until 1919.
Ghent: Exposition Universelle et Internationale.

1914 Deutsche Werkbund exhibition in Cologne.
Paris: Exposition de l'Art Décoratif de la Grande-Bretagne et d'Irlande. Held at the Louvre, and organised by the Board of Trade, the exhibition featured the work of all the leading Arts and Crafts artists.

1915 Gustav Stickley enterprises declared bankrupt.
Alice and Elbert Hubbard perish on the Lusitania, 7th May.
Founding of the Design and Industries Association. Many of the leading Arts and Crafts figures were instrumental in its formation, including Harry Peach of the Dryad Workshops, Harold Stabler, Selwyn Image, W. A. S. Benson, W. R. Lethaby and Ambrose Heal.
San Francisco: Panama-Pacific International Exposition.
San Diego: Panama-Californian Exposition.

1916 Last issue of *Philopolis*, September.
Last issue of *The Craftsman*, December.

1919 The Bauhaus founded in April in Weimar by Walter Gropius, who had studied architecture under Peter Behrens.

1 MORRIS AND HIS CIRCLE

Two great thinkers, Morris and Ruskin, tower above all the rest in the nineteenth century when questions of art and aesthetics are being considered. John Ruskin is regarded as the most important influence on the progress of design in the second half of the nineteenth century. As Kenneth Clark has pointed out he was the most widely read writer in the English language and the most influential of the new social critics. For Morris, Ruskin's ideal of mediaeval life encapsulated his own developing socialist theories. Ruskin himself might have been surprised to learn that 'Tolstoy, Gandhi and Bernard Shaw, to name only three, believed him to be one of the greatest social reformers of his time.'[1] Ruskin's predictably antipathetic reactions to Paxton's Crystal Palace show him to have supported, albeit unconsciously, the socialist rejection of officialdom in art. It expressed, he wrote, 'a single and very admirable thought of Sir Joseph Paxton's . . . that it might be possible to build a greenhouse larger than had ever been built before. This thought, and some very ordinary algebra, are as much as all that glass can represent of human intellect'.[2]

If Ruskin was mainly influential through his writings, Morris taught by the example of his enthusiasm; the availability of the products of Morris and Co., and the accessibility of his writings both in England and America made his ideas easy to absorb. But above all he inspired emulation through the wide range of his personal contacts — it is probably true to say that there was hardly an English artist of importance connected with the movement who had not met him, or any American who had not read him; indeed, personal memories and letters of the period reveal how many Americans had also met him. It is for this reason that he is regarded as the father of the movement rather than for any true originality in his designs. It is significant that by 1890 the furniture designed for Morris and Co. by George Jack, Mervyn Macartney and W. A. S. Benson was essentially eighteenth century pastiche, both in technique and style, a revealing departure from the solidity of Philip Webb's mediaevalising manner of the early period.

From the time when the industrial revolution had put machinery at the disposal of the manufacturers of all kinds of goods, including the silversmith and the jeweller, artists had increasingly withdrawn from the commercial arena leaving the

58 William De Morgan – Tile panel, early Fulham period, c. 1889.

---

1 Kenneth Clark *Ruskin Today*, p. xiii.
2 John Ruskin *The Stones of Venice* I, appendix XVII.

mass-production of novelties and trinkets in sham materials and by short-cut techniques to the aesthetically uneducated. Pevsner speaks of the demand for these mass-produced goods emanating from 'an uneducated and debased population, living in slave-filth and penury'.[3] While no-one would dispute the penury of the nineteenth century working class population, the fact remains that much of the demand for mass-produced decorative objects came from the far from slave-filthy middle classes whose untroubled affluence has become a byword in the modern day. Morris and his followers in the craft revival movement were later to discover to their chagrin that their attempts to bring sweetness, light and art into the lives of the working classes were supported almost exclusively by the middle classes whom many might stigmatise as being in as much need of aesthetic education as any 'honest working man'. In claiming that he did not want 'art for the few', Morris was, unconsciously, recommending mass-production, the only means by which this worthy ideal could possibly be realised. The only practical aim was — to paraphrase Walter Crane — to 'turn our artists into manufacturers and our manufacturers into artists', an altogether more realistic ideal which was, to a certain extent, forwarded by the foundation of the Deutsche Werkbund and the Design and Industries Association (D.I.A.). It is to the eternal credit of a few tireless pioneers that this trend towards a totally divided artistic point of view had been halted and the rift between art and commerce partially healed by the final decade of the nineteenth century.

WILLIAM MORRIS (1834–1896)

English artist, poet, designer and craftsman
William Morris was born in Walthamstow, the son of a prosperous bill-broker, and was educated at Marlborough and at Exeter College, Oxford. In 1853, when he was up at Oxford, he met Edward Burne-Jones, the artist, who was to become his life-long friend. In 1855, while on holiday with Burne-Jones, Morris decided to abandon his intention of entering the Church and to devote his life to art instead — through the practice of architecture. He entered the office of G. E. Street, at that time established in Oxford, in January 1856. There he met Street's chief assistant, Philip Webb, who was later to design Morris's house and to collaborate with him in the setting up of Morris and Co. Under the influence of Rossetti Morris gave up his architectural studies at the end of 1856 in order to take up painting, and assisted Rossetti in the scheme for decorating the Oxford Union Library in 1857. His career as a painter was short-lived, and during the next two years he came, through a process of trial and error, to realise his true vocation — that of pattern designer — for which he showed a talent amounting to genius, and which he utilised for creating wallpapers, fabrics, book decorations and designs for tapestry weaving.

3 Nicholas Pevsner *Pioneers of the Modern Movement*, Chapter 1.

59

I once a king and chief · now am the tree-barks thief :

ever twixt trunk and leaf · chasing the prey ·

60

59 Morris and Co. – 'The Woodpecker'. Wool tapestry designed by William Morris and woven at Merton Abbey, 1885.

60 Morris and Co. – Silk and wool carpet, c. 1880.

Page 66
61 William Morris – Embroidered crewel-work hanging, designed in 1877, worked by Mrs Ada Phoebe Godman for Smeaton Manor, built in 1876 by Philip Webb.

In 1859 the designs for the Red House were put in hand by Philip Webb, and by the autumn of 1860 the house was ready for occupation. The completed house demanded very special treatment for the interior decoration and furnishing. Nothing that could be bought ready-made pleased Morris, and eventually much of the furniture was designed by Philip Webb and executed under his direct supervision. The decorating was undertaken by Morris and his friends Rossetti and Burne-Jones. His experience of the frustrations which confronted him while setting up house convinced Morris that he should found his own decorating firm. Thus in April 1861 Morris, Marshall, Faulkner and Co. was formed, just in time to prepare an exhibit to be shown at the International Exhibition in the following year. Morris's influence on the decorative arts of the second half of the nineteenth century can hardly be overestimated. This influence was exercised chiefly through the firm, with his lectures on pattern making and craft techniques, such as tapestry weaving, acting as a further stimulus to the craft revival movement.

Wallpapers, the first dating from 1862, were amongst the earliest products of the firm, along with Philip Webb's furniture and the stained glass designs of Rossetti, Burne-Jones and Ford Madox Brown. The wallpapers were printed by Jeffrey and Co. Morris began designing fabrics in the late 1860s, the first experiments with vegetable dyes dating from 1875, and being made in conjunction with Thomas Wardle of Leek in Staffordshire. After the acquisition of the Merton Abbey Tapestry Works in 1881, Morris decided to undertake the printing himself and the first chintzes were produced there in 1883. The first tapestry weaving experiments date from 1879, and in 1880 Morris embarked on the weaving of hand-knotted rugs in Hammersmith. In 1890 he set up his last venture, the Kelmscott Press, which was to obsess him for the few remaining years of his life. He died at Kelmscott House, Hammersmith, in 1896 at the age of sixty-two.

PHILIP WEBB (1831–1915)

British architect and designer

Born in Oxford, Webb was apprenticed to the Reading architect, John Billing, in 1849. In 1852 he became chief assistant to G. E. Street, whose office was then in Oxford. In 1856 William Morris joined the firm as a pupil, and in the summer of the same year Street moved the office to London, accompanied by both Webb and Morris. Morris only stayed on in the office for a few months, but Webb remained with Street until 1859 when he set up in practice on his own. One of his first commissions as an independent architect was the designing and building of the Red House at Upton in Kent for Morris. Ultimately much of the furniture for the house was

Page 67
62 Edward Burne-Jones – 'The Failure of Sir Gawain'. Detail from a tapestry hanging, one of the series of the 'Holy Grail', designed for Stanmore Hall and woven at Merton Abbey, 1894.

Opposite above
63 Edward Burne-Jones – Tapestry hanging, one of the series of the 'Holy Grail', designed for Stanmore Hall and woven at Merton Abbey, 1894.

Opposite below
64 Morris and Co. –
(left) 'Blackthorn' wallpaper, 1892;
65 *(right)* 'Cray' chintz, 1884.

designed by Webb and made under his anxious supervision, so he was inevitably drawn into the decorating firm which was founded by Morris a year after the Red House was completed.

Much of the furniture for Morris and Co. in the early years was designed by Webb, and his style was widely influential on the craft revival designers of the 1880s and 1890s. He designed a number of country houses, including 'Clouds' at East Knoyle in Wiltshire for the Hon. Percy Wyndham, which was decorated by Morris and Co. One of his last major commissions was the designing of 'Standen' near East Grinstead, which has remained almost miraculously untouched and is preserved, furnished as far as possible as Webb would have intended, by the National Trust.

66 Richard Norman Shaw – Oak chair designed for the Tabard Inn, Bedford Park, 1876. This design was also sold through Morris and Co.

MORRIS AND COMPANY

British furnishing and decorating firm

Morris and Company was founded under the name of Morris, Marshall, Faulkner and Co. in April 1861, at 8 Red Lion Square. The firm moved in 1865 to 26 Queen Square, and was reorganised in 1875 as Morris and Co., with William Morris as sole proprietor. In 1877 showrooms were acquired in Oxford Street, and in 1881 the workshops were moved to Merton Abbey. In the 1920s the showrooms were moved to Hanover Square and the firm finally went into voluntary liquidation in 1940.

The early designs for furniture for the firm were provided by Philip Webb and Ford Madox Brown; later many of the designs were commissioned from George Jack, who became the firm's chief designer in 1890, as well as W. A. S. Benson and Mervyn Macartney. The famous 'Sussex' chairs were based on a traditional pattern. They became one of the most influential products of the firm and were copied in many different versions well into the present century. Important decorative commissions undertaken by the firm included the Armoury and Tapestry Room at St. James's Palace; the Green Dining Room at the South Kensington Museum; the Earl of Carlisle's house at 1 Palace Green; Alexander Ionides' house at Holland Park in London; Rounton Grange, Northallerton for Sir Lowthian Bell; 'Clouds', East Knoyle, in Wiltshire for the Hon. Percy Wyndham and Stanmore Hall for W. Knox d'Arcy.

WILLIAM FREND DE MORGAN (1839–1917)

British artist, potter and novelist

William De Morgan was born in London, the son of a distinguished mathematician and astronomer, and entered the Royal Academy Schools in 1859 with the intention of studying

67 William De Morgan – Design for a vase, c. 1890.

to become an artist. In the early 1860s he was introduced into the Pre-Raphaelite circle. He met William Morris and Burne-Jones through his fellow Academy student, Henry Holiday, and they inevitably encountered Rossetti, Madox Brown, Woolner the sculptor, and Morris's friends Charles Faulkner and Cornell Prince at Burne-Jones' studio.

Very soon after becoming a member of this circle De Morgan abandoned his artistic ambitions in favour of a career in decorative design, and began working for Morris and Co. — recently established by Morris and his friends in Red Lion Square — designing stained glass and tiles. Disliking the way in which his designs were reproduced, he decided to set up a kiln in the basement of his own home in Fitzroy Square, where he continued to produce tiles and stained glass for Morris. In the early 1870s, by his own account, he 'rediscovered' the lost art of lustre decoration for pottery. He later became aware of the fact that the art had already been revived in Italy in the mid-1850s and firmly repudiated the claims made on his behalf to be the true originator of this method of decoration. In the course of his experiments with the lustre decorating technique a fierce flame from the kiln set the chimney on fire and the roof of the Fitzroy Square house was destroyed.

After the death of his father in 1871, De Morgan moved with his mother and sister, in 1872, to 30 Cheyne Row, which he used as showroom, studio and workshop. He was assisted here with the painting of the tiles and the hollow-wares by Charles and Fred Passenger, who remained with him for thirty and twenty-eight years respectively. Later they were joined by an accomplished artist, Joe Juster, who produced some of the finest work of the firm.

In 1881 De Morgan transferred the business to Merton Abbey to be near Morris's new workshops, but the journey to and from London damaged his already precarious health and in 1888 he transferred his workshop and kiln again, this time to Sands End, Fulham, where he went into partnership with Halsey Ricardo, the architect. In 1885 he married a fellow artist, Evelyn Pickering, who was to exert a considerable influence on him in his later career. The partnership with Ricardo ended in 1898, and De Morgan carried on at Fulham in partnership with the Passenger brothers and Frank Iles until he retired from active participation in the business in 1905. The partnership ended in 1907. From 1892 onwards he spent a considerable amount of his time in Florence, and during that period some of his designs were used by the Italian pottery firm of Cantigalli. In the later years of his life he turned seriously to writing fiction, and became well-known as a novelist of distinction.

HENRY GEORGE ALEXANDER HOLIDAY (1839–1927)

British artist and designer

Holiday trained at the Royal Academy Schools which he attended from the age of fifteen, exhibiting at the Royal Academy for the first time in 1857. He was a fellow student of Simeon Solomon, William De Morgan, and W. Richmond and through them was drawn into the orbit of Pre-Raphaelitism. He was noticed early in his career by Holman Hunt who saw him as a promising member of the new generation of Academy students. He joined Powells of Whitefriars, the glass manufacturers, as a stained glass cartoonist — in succession to Burne-Jones — and designed some of their richest and finest work.

Although Pre-Raphaelite in derivation, his glass windows are recognisable on account of a freedom of handling and pictorial organisation which breaks away from the cramped perspective and enclosed framework of early Morris & Co. glass designs. He also designed mosaics, enamels and embroideries (often worked by his wife Catherine who also executed a number of embroidered panels for Morris & Co.), and worked on mural painting.

68 W.A.S. Benson – Copper and brass table lamp, c. 1890.

MAY MORRIS (1862–1938)

British designer, embroideress and craft jeweller

May was the youngest daughter of William Morris from whom she received her artistic education. She designed textiles and wallpapers for Morris and Co., and executed a number of embroidery commissions for the firm including ecclesiastical work. She managed the embroidery workshop at Merton Abbey from 1886 and was a founder member of the Women's Guild of Arts in 1907, later becoming chairman. In 1910 she lectured in America on design and embroidery. She designed and made a small number of pieces of jewellery, and made a speciality of bead necklaces. After her father's death May Morris took on the mammoth task of editing his complete writings, which appeared in twenty-four volumes between 1910 and 1914.

WILLIAM ARTHUR SMITH BENSON (1854–1924)

British metalworker and furniture designer

W. A. S. Benson was born in London and was educated at Winchester and Oxford (1874–8) where he met Morris and Burne-Jones and shared lodgings with Heywood Sumner. In 1878 he was articled to the architect Basil Champneys but in 1880, encouraged by Morris, he opened a small workshop in

69 W.A.S. Benson – Copper oil lamp, *c.* 1890.

Hammersmith, specialising in metalwork. In 1882 he moved to larger premises in Chiswick and in 1887 opened showrooms in Bond Street. During the 1880s he was involved in designing wallpapers and cabinet-making for Morris and Co., making silver mounts and hinges; he also designed furniture for J. S. Henry & Co. which specialised in Art Nouveau furniture. He became a director of Morris and Co. after Morris' death in 1896 although he still maintained his own workshops where he specialised in designing metalwork for mass-production.

Benson was a founder of the Art-Workers' Guild in 1884 and in 1888 encouraged the foundation of the Arts and Crafts Exhibition Society with a scheme for the exhibition of 'The Combined Arts'. In 1915 he was among the founder members of the D.I.A. The metalwork from his Eyot works in Chiswick was often featured in *The Studio* and was also sold at Samuel Bing's shop *L'Art Nouveau* in Paris. He retired from business in 1920.

GEORGE JACK (1855–1932)

British architect and designer

George Jack was born in Long Island, U.S.A., and was articled to the Glasgow architect Horatio K. Bromhead in the early 1870s. He came to London in 1875, and after working for five years for another London architect he entered the office of Philip Webb in 1880. He became chief furniture designer to Morris and Co. in 1890 and was responsible for many of the quasi-eighteenth century pieces carried out in mahogany with inlaid decoration which present such a contrast to Webb's early designs for the firm. In 1900 he took over Philip Webb's architectural practice.

70 Morris and Co. showrooms at 449 Oxford Street.

71

71 Philip Webb – 'The Red House', designed for William Morris, 1859.

72 D.G. Rossetti – 'St. George and the Dragon' stained glass panel made by Morris and Co., *c*. 1861.

72

the joyful Princess was borne home again

73

75

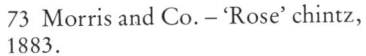

73 Morris and Co. – 'Rose' chintz, 1883.

74 Morris and Co. – 'Wey' chintz, 1883.

75 Morris and Co. – 'Borage' chintz block. Metal on a wooden base, 10½ × 9 ins., 1883.

74

THE SUSSEX RUSH-SEATED CHAIRS
MORRIS AND COMPANY
449 OXFORD STREET, LONDON, W.

"ROSSETTI ARM-CHAIR.
IN BLACK, 16/6.

SUSSEX CORNER CHAIR.
IN BLACK, 10/6.

SUSSEX SINGLE CHAIR.
IN BLACK, 7/-.

SUSSEX ARM-CHAIR.
IN BLACK, 9/9.

ROUND-SEAT CHAIR.
IN BLACK, 10/6.

SUSSEX SETTEE, 4 FT. 6 IN. LONG.
IN BLACK, 35/-.

ROUND SEAT PIANO CHAIR.
IN BLACK, 10/6.

76

76 Page of chairs from Morris and Co. catalogue, c. 1910. These chairs were produced throughout the whole of the firm's existence, and copied by many other firms, notably Heal and Sons.

77 Morris and Co. – The 'Sussex' triple seat settee.

78 D.G. Rossetti – Stained oak 'Rossetti' chair, made by Morris and Co.

79 Ford Madox Brown – Stained chair with rush seat, made by Morris and Co.

77

78

79

80

80 George Jack – Dining table for Morris and Co., *c.* 1890.

81 Page from Morris and Co. catalogue, *c.* 1910. The line drawings usually show items designed in the early years of the firm.

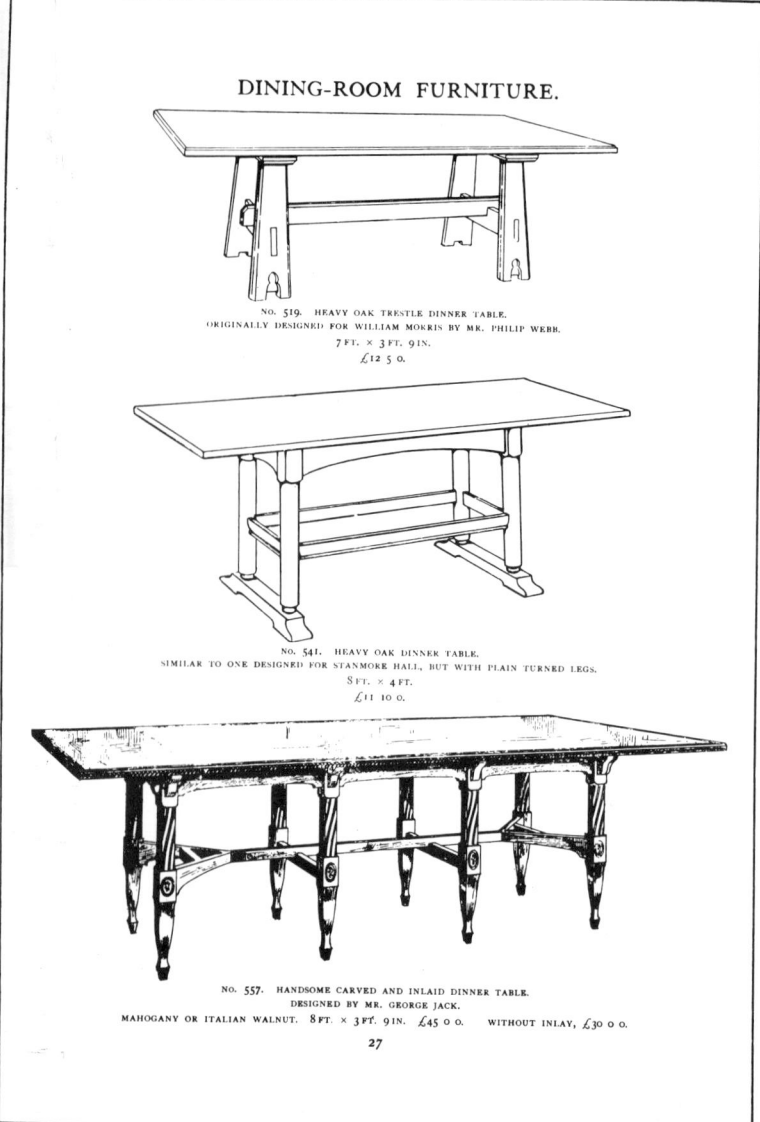

DINING-ROOM FURNITURE.

NO. 519. HEAVY OAK TRESTLE DINNER TABLE.
ORIGINALLY DESIGNED FOR WILLIAM MORRIS BY MR. PHILIP WEBB.
7 FT. × 3 FT. 9 IN.
£12 5 0.

NO. 541. HEAVY OAK DINNER TABLE.
SIMILAR TO ONE DESIGNED FOR STANMORE HALL, BUT WITH PLAIN TURNED LEGS.
8 FT. × 4 FT.
£11 10 0.

NO. 557. HANDSOME CARVED AND INLAID DINNER TABLE.
DESIGNED BY MR. GEORGE JACK.
MAHOGANY OR ITALIAN WALNUT. 8 FT. × 3 FT. 9 IN. £45 0 0. WITHOUT INLAY, £30 0 0.

27

81

82 Morris and Co. – Stanmore Hall dining-room for William Knox d'Arcy, the fireplace and panelling by W.R. Lethaby, 1889.

83 Morris and Co. catalogue, *c.* 1910. Stanmore Hall dining-room, showing the Burne-Jones tapestry *in situ*.

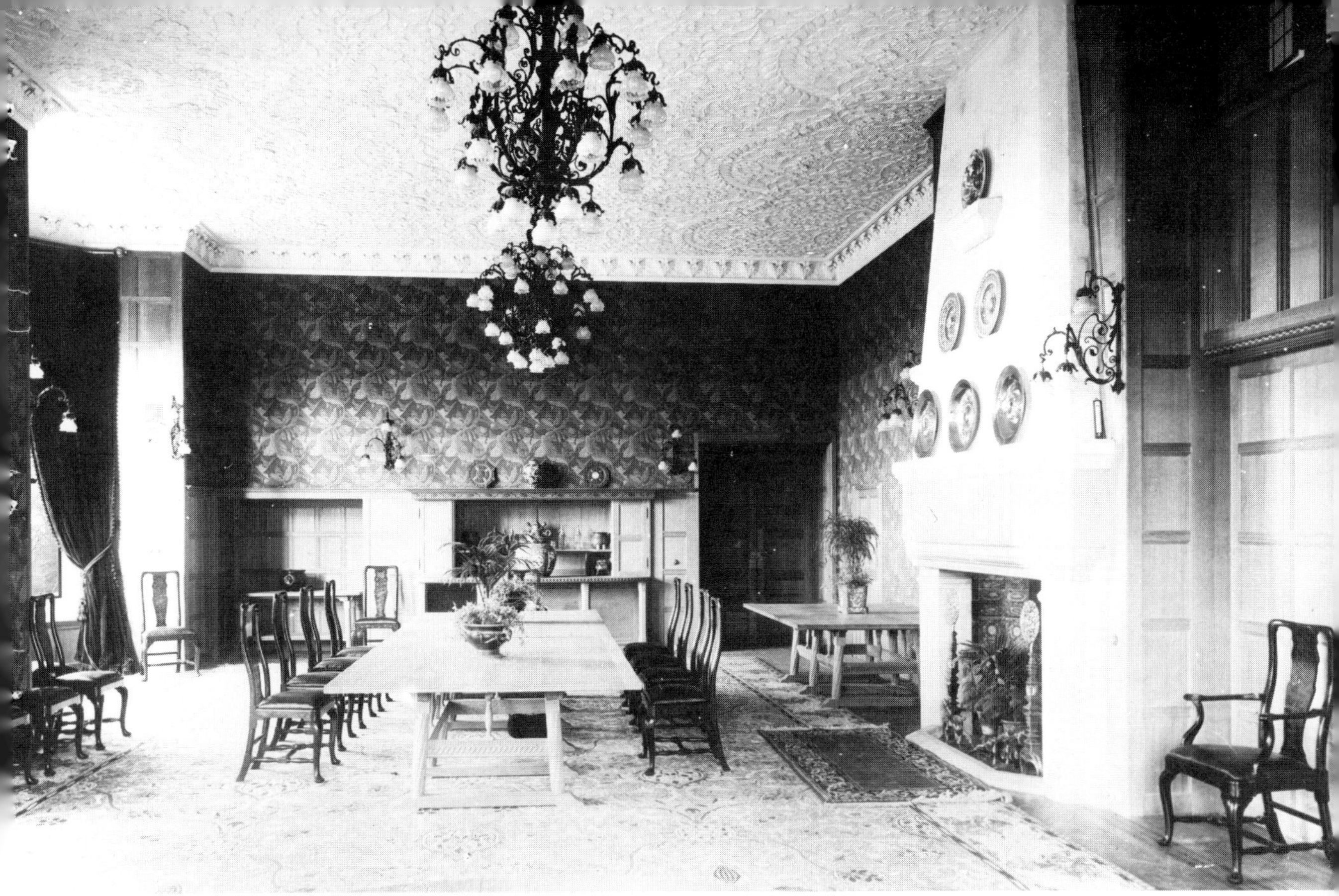

82

83

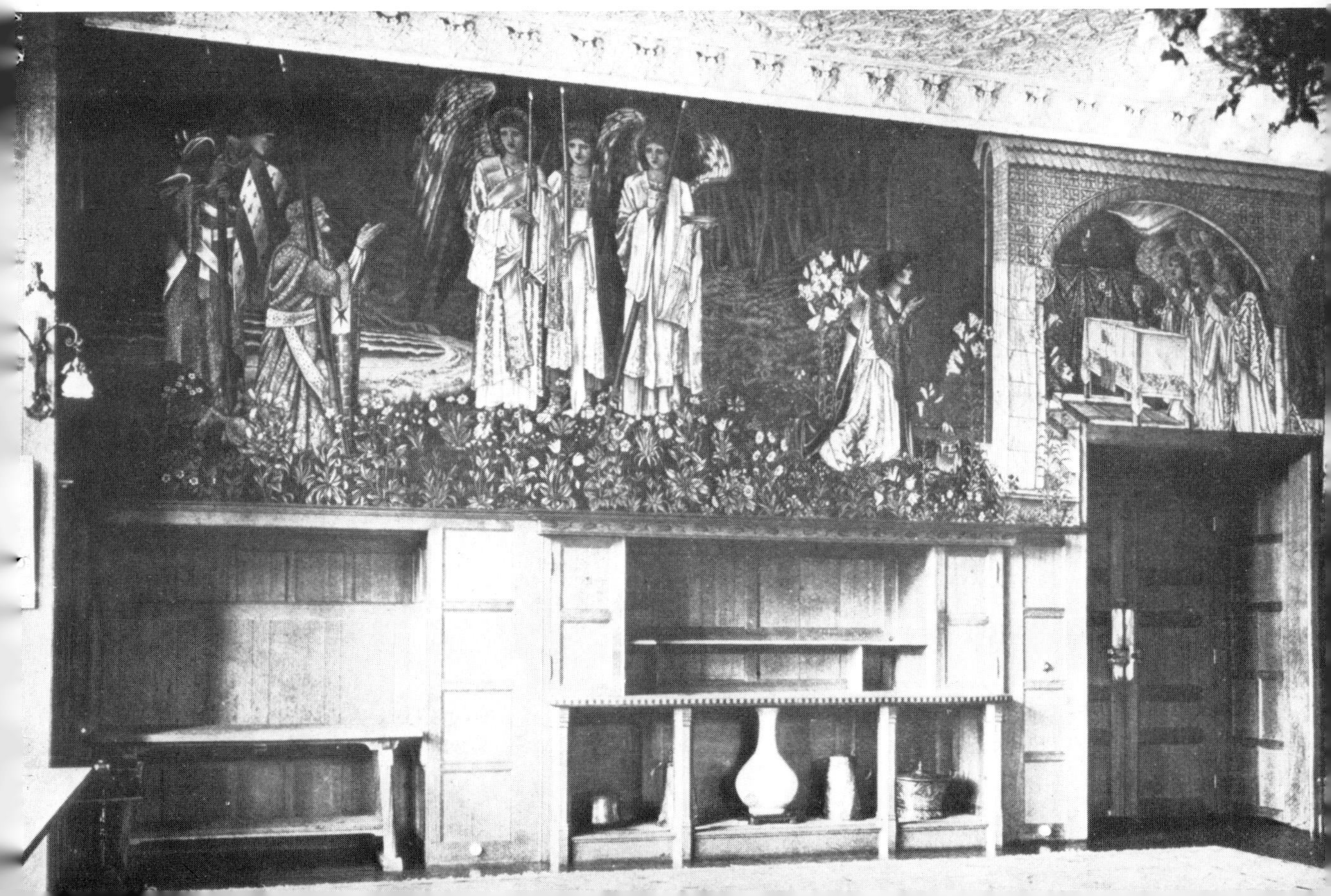

NO. 565. OAK SETTLE, DESIGNED BY MR. PHILIP WEBB.

PANELS DECORATED WITH EMBOSSED LEATHER PAPER — £35 0 0
WITH PLAIN OAK PANELS — £30 0 0

84 Kelmscott House, Hammersmith. Interior after Morris's death.

85 Page from Morris and Co. catalogue, c. 1910.

86 Page from Morris and Co. catalogue, c. 1910.

GOTHIC SIDEBOARD. DESIGNED BY MR. PHILIP WEBB,
AND MADE BY MORRIS AND COMPANY IN THE EARLIEST DAYS OF THE FIRM AT RED LION SQUARE (C. 1862).

87 William De Morgan – Design for a vase, c. 1890.

88 William De Morgan – Panel of eight tiles, painted in colours, early Fulham period, 1887-89.

89 William De Morgan – Lustre dish, painted by Fred Passenger, 14 in. diameter, late Fulham period, 1898-1907.

90 William De Morgan – Lustre dish, painted by Fred Passenger, 14 in. diameter, late Fulham period, 1898-1907.

87

88

89

90

91 Philip Webb – One of a pair of
copper candlesticks, 10½ in. high,
c. 1861.

92 W.A.S. Benson – Copper and
brass table lamp, sold by Morris and
Co., c. 1890.

92

2 'TOWARDS A FREE STYLE'

Morris did not succeed in either formulating a truly new design principle or in releasing the decorative arts from the stifling grip of Puginesque historicism. Norman Shaw, W. R. Lethaby and H. H. Richardson, having absorbed the ideals behind the initial impetus towards purity of form, then went forward to create a stylistic framework within which the movement could expand. In achieving a break with the grandiloquent manner of High Victorian architecture and decoration, these architects developed a vernacular style in design which brought with it a movement towards a democratic art as embodied, for instance, in the concept of the garden city.

Whereas Morris is regarded as the source of ideals, in America — at least — C. L. Eastlake had provided the pattern-book for the Gothic style, a necessary starting point for stylistic reform. This was largely misinterpreted in use because the Americans had not had an identifiable Gothic Revival of their own from which to draw the ideology inspiring *Hints on Household Taste*, and the 'Eastlake style' is not based on any radical rethinking of basic premises about the structure and decoration of furniture. The resulting misuse of Eastlake's patterns could thus lead straight into the craft revival style without the need to unload the by now stale Ruskinian ideas which had hampered the search for a pure form.

L. C. Tiffany not only adopted the ideals of Morris — he wished to create, in his studio, a cross between the European atelier and the Morrisian guild — but also the more lavish aesthetic concepts put into practice by Rohlfs and Sullivan.

RICHARD NORMAN SHAW
(1831–1912)

British architect and designer
After training in the office of William Burn, Shaw became chief assistant to G. E. Street in 1859 in succession to Philip Webb. In 1862 he set up in practice with W. E. Nesfield. He was commissioned to design houses for the garden suburb developed by Jonathan Carr at Bedford Park in 1877/78, to replace designs provided by E. W. Godwin which were abandoned as unsatisfactory. As well as working at his extensive and successful architectural practice Norman Shaw

Opposite
93 L.C. Tiffany – Dome for a garden room in stained and iridescent glass, *c.* 1900.

Page 86
94 Louis C. Tiffany – Group of iridescent glasses, 1900-1912.

95 Louis C. Tiffany – Panel of stained glass designed for a garden room, *c.* 1900.

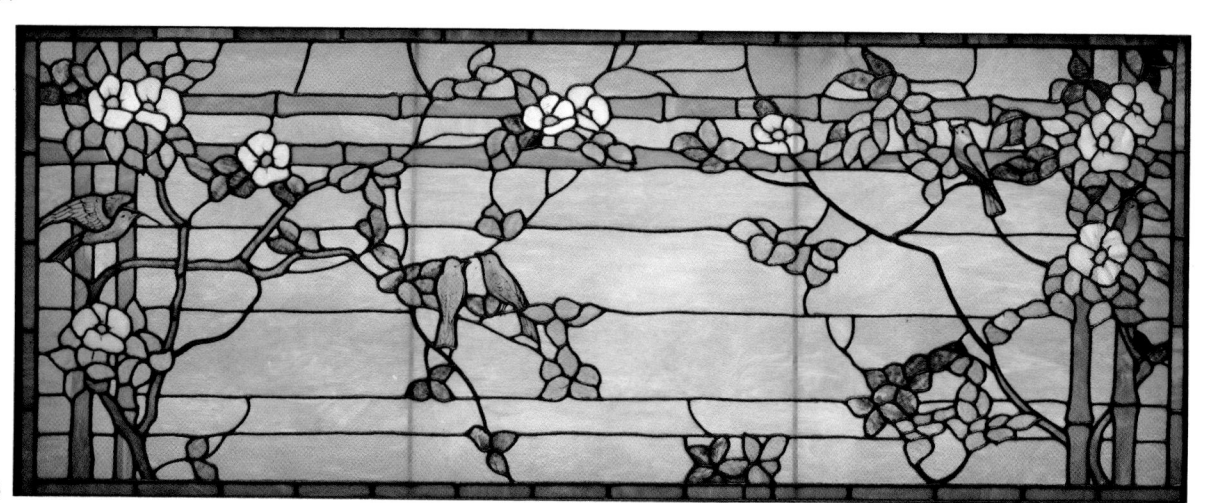

94

95

made designs for furniture and wallpapers. Some of the furniture designs combine the massive quality of Morris at his most Gothic with the decorative quality of Burges, and they provide a logical link between Puginesque Gothic and Gimson's craft tradition furniture. Two of Gimson's partners in the cabinet making firm, Kenton & Company (q.v.) were pupils of Norman Shaw.

HENRY HOBSON RICHARDSON (1838–86)

American architect and interior designer

Richardson was educated at Harvard and the Ecole des Beaux-Arts in Paris. After working in Paris he began working as an architect in New York, moving to Massachusetts in 1874. He introduced an element of Romanticism into American architecture, known as 'Richardson Romanesque', perhaps best typified by his Trinity Church, Boston (1872–77), which marked a departure from a Gothic revival style. He worked with Augustus Saint Gaudens and the stained glass designer John La Farge on his interiors. He designed the building for the Marshall Field Wholesale Store in Chicago which stocked Morris and Co. goods.

DANIEL PABST (1826–1910)

American furniture designer and decorator

Pabst was born 11 June 1826 in Hesse-Darmstadt, settled in Philadelphia in 1849 and opened his own shop in July 1854, becoming the most well-known of many German furniture makers. His workshop employed up to fifty men. He won an award for a sideboard at the Centennial Exhibition, Philadelphia in 1876, and he may have been influenced by Christopher Dresser who lectured there that year. There is evidence to show a possible association with the architect Frank Furness. Around 1875 his style changed from being predominantly Renaissance to absorb the influences of the Gothic Revival and also, after 1876, the Aesthetic Movement. Pabst died 15 July 1910.

HERTER BROTHERS

Interior designers and silversmiths

Gustave and Christian Herter were born in Stuttgart and settled in America in the late 1840s. Gustave worked as a silver designer for Tiffany's and then founded his own firm in New York in the 1850s. Christian, who produced most of the designs, trained in Paris and joined his half-brother's firm, which then became known as Herter Brothers, in the

Page 87
96 L.C. Tiffany – Stained glass panel, showing a landscape (detail of the centre panel from a triptych), *c.* 1910.

Opposite
97 L.C. Tiffany – Lamp with a leaded glass shade and a bronze base, *c.* 1900.

mid-1860s. Christian returned to Paris in the late 1860s and his designs of the 1870s and early 1880s reflect the Japanese taste. They designed interiors for Jay Gould, J. P. Morgan, Lillian Russell, Mark Hopkins and W. H. Vanderbilt among others.

CHELSEA KERAMIC ART WORKS

American art pottery company

The company had been formed in 1866 in Massachusetts producing common brown ware and in 1872 Alexander W. Robertson, his brothers George and Hugh, and his father James began to produce art pottery, using ancient Greek forms in terracotta. After seeing the Oriental pottery at ·the Philadelphia Centennial in 1876, Chelsea faience was introduced using the 'Limoges' underglaze for their wares, which were known as 'Bourg-la-Reine'. Hugh C. Robertson also began experimenting with Oriental glazes — peachblow, celadon and sang-de-boeuf.

In 1880 the father, James Robertson, died. George had already left in 1878 with the firm's decorator, John G. Low, to form the J. and J. G. Low Art Tile Works, and in 1884 Alexander left for California. Hugh spent so much time perfecting his sang-de-boeuf that in 1888 production ceased due to lack of funds. In 1891 the Chelsea Pottery was formed with Hugh as manager and he then produced a best-selling line of crackled ware. The pottery was moved to Dedham in 1896, to become the Dedham Pottery. In 1904 they won an award at the St. Louis World's Fair. Hugh died in 1908 and his son continued the business until it closed in 1943.

MARY LOUISE McLAUGHLIN
(1847–1937)

American ceramist

M. L. McLaughlin worked with the Cincinnati Pottery Club and formed the Women's Pottery Club in 1879. She was especially known for her use of the 'Limoges' underglaze decoration which had been developed by E. Chaplet, whose work she saw at the Philadelphia Centennial of 1876. Her work was known as 'Cincinnati Limoges'. In 1878 she exhibited both in New York and the World's Fair in Paris. In 1882, when Rookwood closed its doors to amateurs, she was forced to abandon her work on underglaze painting but continued to write and work within the decorative arts. In 1895 she returned to ceramics, working with inlaid decoration and in 1898 turned her attention to high-fired white porcelain, known as Losanti ware, which she exhibited widely between 1901 and 1904. In 1906 she finally abandoned ceramics completely.

98 Rookwood Pottery – Pottery tile, 4½ × 8¾ in., 1910-11.

ROOKWOOD POTTERY

American pottery company

Rookwood was founded in 1880 by Maria Longworth Nichols (Storer). Mrs Nichols had connections with the Cincinnati Pottery Club and until 1883 the Woman's Pottery Club used their kilns and several of its members continued to design for Rookwood. In 1884 the 'Standard' Rookwood ware was introduced by Laura Fry using the Limoges underglaze painting technique for which the company was best known although from 1881 some printed ware was also produced. Mrs Nichols herself was mainly intrigued by Oriental pottery and used many Japanese motifs and shapes in her 'Nancy' ware.

Several renowned ceramists worked for Rookwood, including Artus Van Briggle (until 1899), William P. MacDonald (from 1882 until his death), Albert Valentien (until 1905; he and his wife subsequently opened their own pottery in California), John D. Wareham and William Watts Taylor who was employed as manager in 1883 and established Rookwood on more commercial lines, although the firm always retained its own cohesive style with naturalistic renderings of animals and plants. One of the most renowned artists working in this style with underglaze painting was Matthew A. Daly (1860–1937) who was born in Cincinnati, trained at the Cincinnati Art Academy and joined Rookwood in 1882, remaining with them until 1903. Rookwood financed several of their artists to study in France. In 1889 Rookwood pottery was awarded the Gold Medal at the Paris World's Fair. In 1901 at the Pan-American Exposition in Buffalo Rookwood first introduced their matt glazes.

ARTUS VAN BRIGGLE (1869–1904)

American painter, sculptor and ceramist

Born in Felicity, Ohio, Van Briggle studied art at the Cincinnati Academy, supporting himself by painting vases at the Avon Pottery. When that closed in 1887 he joined Rookwood. He still wanted to be a painter, however, and Rookwood financed him to study at the Académie Julian in Paris from 1893 to 1896. In March 1899, suffering from tuberculosis, he resigned from Rookwood and went to Colorado where, by 1901, he had established his own small studio. There he began to absorb Art Nouveau forms, as in his 'Lorelei' vase. In 1903 he began exhibiting and won several medals at the 1904 Louisiana Purchase International Exposition, although he died before learning this. His wife enlarged the pottery in 1907 and it still continues today. Van Briggle was an exponent of combining the arts of sculpture and ceramics in his work.

ALEXANDER FISHER (1864–1936)

British sculptor, silversmith and enamellist

Fisher studied at the South Kensington Schools and then in France and Italy on a travelling scholarship. On his return to England he set up his own workshop. From 1896 to 1899 he taught at the Central School of Arts and Crafts. He set up a short-lived partnership with Henry Wilson (q.v.) whom he had met at the Central School, but irrevocable temperamental differences between the two men doomed it to failure. He exhibited a number of pieces, including his 'Wagnerian' girdle, at the house of his pupil, the Honorable Mrs Percy Wyndham, in Belgrave Square in 1899. He set up his own school of enamelling at his studio in Warwick Gardens in 1904.

Fisher wrote extensively on the craft of enamelling in *The Studio*. His work was to influence the many artists involved in the enamelling revival at the turn of the century, notably that of his pupils such as Ernestine Mills and Mrs Percy Wyndham, as well as the enamellists of the Birmingham School, notably Mr and Mrs Arthur Gaskin and Sidney Meteyarde and his wife Kate M. Eadie. He was indirectly responsible for the stylistic trend of Mrs Nelson Dawson (q.v.), and much of the formal structure of Phoebe Traquair's work is closely related to his own, though the range of colour in the enamels is rather different. Fisher is a perfect example of the influential, artist-craftsman disseminating his ideas through his work, his teaching and his writing, and presents an interesting contrast with Ruskin, whose enormous influence stemmed from his writing alone, and Morris, whose style was popularised through the activities of 'the firm' and through lecturing.

99 Martin Bros. – Stoneware jug in the form of a monster, 1880.

THE MARTIN BROTHERS

British art pottery company

This pottery firm was established in London by the four Martin brothers in 1873, when the eldest, Robert Wallace (born 1843), set up his workshop and studio in Pomona House, King's Road, Fulham, where he was assisted by his three younger brothers Charles, Walter and Edwin. R. W. Martin trained as a sculptor, working for some months with J. B. Philip, and later as a sculptor's assistant on the carvings for A. W. N. Pugin's new Houses of Parliament. He studied at the Lambeth School of Art and at the Royal Academy Schools before going to work for the Pre-Raphaelite sculptor, Alexander Monro, and his own work was exhibited at the Royal Academy sporadically between 1863 and 1872. He began working as a potter in 1871, and in 1872 went to work for C. J. C. Bailey at his Fulham Pottery. In 1873 he set up on his own account with his three brothers.

Both Walter and Edwin Martin studied at the Lambeth School of Art and the two of them also worked as boy assistants in the Doulton Studio. Walter later became the principal thrower and Edwin the principal decorator of their own firm, while Charles Martin took over the business arrangements and had charge of the shop which was opened in Brownlow Street near High Holborn in 1879. In 1877 a suitable site for a kiln and studio was found at Southall in Middlesex and the pottery business was moved there from Pomona House. The pottery remained in Fulham until 1914 when the last firing took place only a few months before Edwin's death. Charles and Walter had already died in 1910 and 1912 respectively. Robert Wallace, the eldest, survived until 1923.

WILLIAM R. LETHABY (1857–1931)

British architect, designer, writer and teacher

Born in Barnstable, Devon, the son of a carver and gilder, Lethaby was articled at an early age to a local architect, Alexander Lauder. In 1877 Lethaby submitted a number of drawings to the newly created 'Designing Club' run by the *Building News*, for which he won the £5 prize. The editor of the magazine continued to publish his drawings, and it was on the strength of these that he was offered the post of chief clerk in Norman Shaw's office in 1879. In 1889 he left Shaw's office to set up on his own. With fellow members of the staff in Shaw's office he promoted first the formation of the Art Workers' Guild and two years later the Arts and Crafts Exhibition Society, of which he was President.

In 1889 he met Ernest Gimson and joined with him in the founding of Kenton and Company, the furniture company which collapsed from lack of capital after only two years. Meanwhile he had begun designing Avon Tyrell for Lord Manners, which was decorated with plasterwork by Gimson and furnished with specially designed furniture made by Kenton and Company. In the same year he provided designs for some of the furniture and interior decorations such as fireplaces and panelling for Stanmore Hall, which was being decorated for William Knox d'Arcy by Morris and Co.

Lethaby joined the Society for the Protection of Ancient Buildings in 1893, and the study of ancient buildings which arose out of work for the Society was to influence his own style from then on. In 1896 he became joint principal with George Frampton, the sculptor, of the newly founded London County Council School of Arts and Crafts. The lettering class there, which was established under the direction of Edward Johnston, arose out of Lethaby's preoccupation with lettering on buildings in which he was a pioneer. He became Master of the Art Workers' Guild in 1911, and was a founder-member of the Design and Industries Association in 1915. He had almost ceased to practise architecture after 1902 as he felt that his training, with its bias towards the study of the great buildings of the past, had not fitted him to design modern scientific buildings in new materials.

CHARLES ROHLFS (1853–1936)

American furniture designer

Rohlfs was born in New York City and trained at the Cooper Union. By 1872 he was designing cast-iron stoves, but later became an actor. In 1890, encouraged by his wife to give up acting, he opened a small workshop in Buffalo where he worked as an independent craftsman, never employing more than eight workmen. The more delicate handiwork was carried out by George Thiele. He exhibited at the International Exhibition of Modern Decorative Arts at Turin in 1902 and was subsequently elected to membership of the Royal Society of Arts in London. He was commissioned to design furniture for Buckingham Palace. He also lectured in East Aurora as a guest of the Roycrofters.

LOUIS HENRY SULLIVAN (1856–1924)

100 Charles Rohlfs – Oak candelabra with copper candle-holders, 1908.

American architect, designer and writer

Born in Boston, Sullivan attended MIT and the Ecole des Beaux-Arts in Paris. On his return from Europe he settled in Chicago and entered the offices of William Le Baron Jenney, who had designed the first steel-skeleton skyscraper. He later entered the office of Dankmar Adler where he became chief draughtsman and, in 1880, a member of the firm. In 1893 his Transportation Building at the Chicago World's Fair heralded his new viewpoint of demonstrating that the outward form of a building should express its function and as such was prominent in the design of business buildings in Chicago.

He had little interest in residential design, although his ideas proved influential on the young architects who worked in his offices, especially Frank Lloyd Wright, who took over much of the non-office design for him. Sullivan opposed traditional design, advocating a functional and truly American style, as expressed in his essays 'Kindergarten Chats', 1918, and his 'Autobiography of an Idea', 1924. Sullivan was the father of what became known as the Prairie School.

LOUIS COMFORT TIFFANY (1848–1933)

American glassmaker and decorator

L. C. Tiffany was the son of Charles Tiffany, the founder of Tiffany & Co., a firm which specialised in silver and jewellery. He studied painting as the sole pupil of George Innes and in

1868–9 travelled in France, Spain and North Africa. He married in 1872 and visited Europe again in 1874. In 1879, with the co-operation of Candace Wheeler, who had been influenced by seeing embroidery from the Kensington School of Art Needlework at the Philadelphia Centennial to found the Society of Decorative Art in New York, he set up Louis C. Tiffany and the Associated Artists. By the early 1880s they were one of the most popular New York decorating firms, on a par with Herter Brothers. In 1882 Oscar Wilde visited their studios and they were commissioned to decorate the White House for President Arthur. In 1885, however, the association with the ladies of Associated Artists foundered and the independent Tiffany Glass Company was formed. That year he moved into the top floor of his father's mansion where he wished to create an atelier akin to the studios of the masters of the Italian Renaissance.

In 1889 Tiffany visited the Paris Exhibition and saw the glass of Emile Gallé; in Paris he also met Samuel Bing and was later to provide stained glass for the opening of his shop in 1895, where the first major exhibition of Tiffany glass was held. In 1892 Tiffany acquired glass furnaces at Corona and the following year the 'Favrile' (meaning 'hand-made') trademark was registered. The first year's production went to museums but the following year, 1895, the first lamps were offered to the public and in 1896 the first Favrile glass was offered for sale. The pottery bases for the lamps, and other items, were purchased from the Grueby Faience Company and the most successful design, for the Wisteria lamp by Mrs Curtis Freschel, was brought out in 1901. Until 1900 the firm was best known for its stained glass and mosaics but after that date the name Tiffany became more associated with the Favrile art glass.

In 1900 the company began producing metalwork, enamelling and bronzes and in 1904 the first pottery from the Corona works was exhibited and first sold the following year. The first glaze was known as 'old ivory'; he also experimented with matt, crystalline and iridescent glazes and in 1911 introduced 'Bronze Pottery', but the work was consistently overshadowed by the virtuosity, in both technique and design, of the Favrile glass. Tiffany himself withdrew from the firm in 1919 but Tiffany Studios continued until 1938.

101 Louis C. Tiffany – Six-light table lamp, c. 1900.

102

103

102, 103 Stanmore Hall – Decorated for William Knox d'Arcy by Morris and Co., 1889, the fire-places and panelling by W.R. Lethaby. The table in the hall (above) possibly designed by Lethaby and made by Kenton & Company.

104 L.C. Tiffany – Iridescent blue 'favrile' vase with stylized peacock feather decoration, c. 1920.

104

105

106

105 *(left)* Martin Brothers – Vase, blue glaze on a dark ground with stylized 'Anthemion' foliage, 1896; *(centre)* Burmantofts Faience – Pear-shaped 'Persian' vase, decorated in the 'Isnik' style, *c.* 1890; *(right)* Pilkington Pottery Co. – 'Royal Lancastrian' vase painted by Gordon M. Forsyth, *c.* 1910.

106 *(left)* Burmantofts Faience – Lime green long-necked vase; *(left centre)* Martin Brothers – Long-necked stoneware vase in the Japanese taste; *(centre)* Martin Brothers – Stoneware jug with painted and incised decoration in the Japanese taste; *(right centre)* Burmantofts Faience – Yellow pear-shaped vase; *(right)* William Moorcroft – 'Florian Ware', two-handled vase decorated with stylized flowers.

107 Herter Bros. – Bed, part of a bedroom set in ebonized cherry with marquetry of lighter woods, showing a Japanese influence, *c.* 1876.

108

109

110

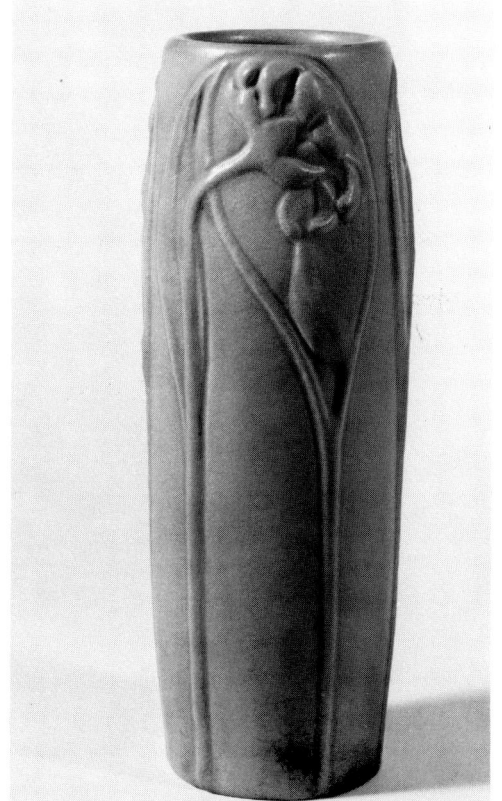

111

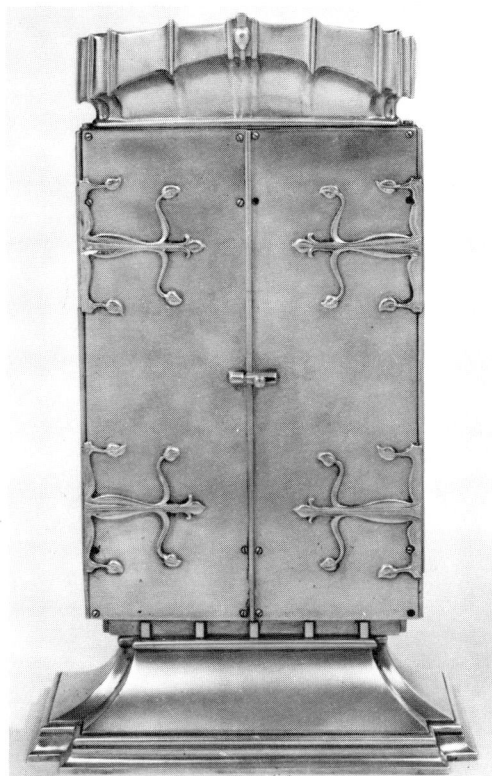

112

113

108 Chelsea Keramic Art Works – Vase, *c.* 1875-80.

109 M. Louise McLaughlin – Earthenware vase with underglaze decoration, 1877.

110 Rookwood Pottery – Vase, 1892.

111 Artus Van Briggle – Glazed pottery vase, 11^{5}/$_{16}$ in. high, 1903.

112 Alexander Fisher – 'The Bridge of Life'. Silver-plated case of enamelled triptych, *c.* 1903.

113 Alexander Fisher – 'The Bridge of Life'. Enamelled triptych, *c.* 1903.

114 Martin Bros. – Stoneware vase with painted decoration.

114

115

115 Charles Rohlfs – Chest of drawers in fumed oak, *c.* 1905.

116 Charles Rohlfs – Oak chair, *c.* 1904.

117

118

117 Louis Sullivan – Lobby of the hotel of the Auditorium Building, Chicago, 1886-90.

118 Candace Wheeler – Printed silk made by Cheney Bros., *c.* 1885. Mrs Wheeler partnered L.C. Tiffany in his early decorative venture, Associated Artists.

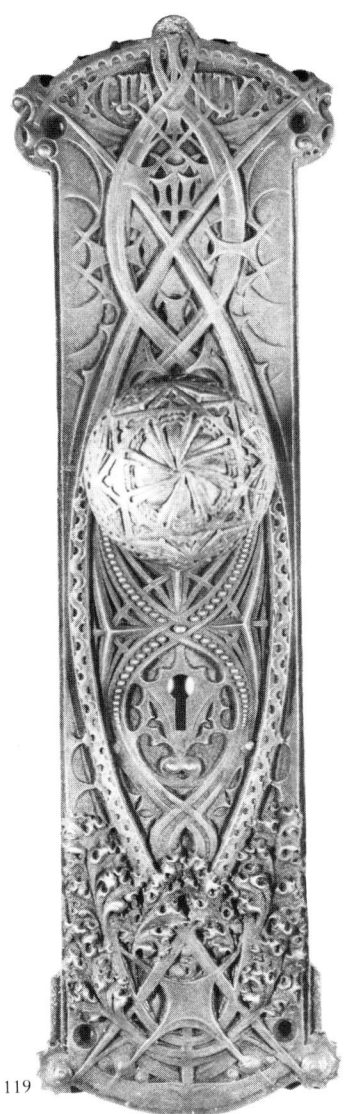

119

119 Louis Sullivan – Door handle and finger plate, cast bronze, Guaranty building, Buffalo, 1894-5.

120 Louis Sullivan – Ornamental ironwork from the front of the Carson, Pirie, Scott store, Chicago, 1899.

120

105

121

122

121 Mrs E. Curtis Freschel – Walnut desk with copper and pewter inlay, *c.* 1904. Mrs Freschel designed Tiffany's famous 'Wisteria' lamp.

122 Tiffany Studios – Bronze box with cast foliate decoration, *c.* 1905.

123

124

123 Louis C. Tiffany – Landscape triptych. Stained glass window, made by Tiffany Studios, 50 × 80½ in., *c.* 1910-19.

124 Louis C. Tiffany – 'Dragonfly' lamp in gilt bronze and leaded glass, *c.* 1900.

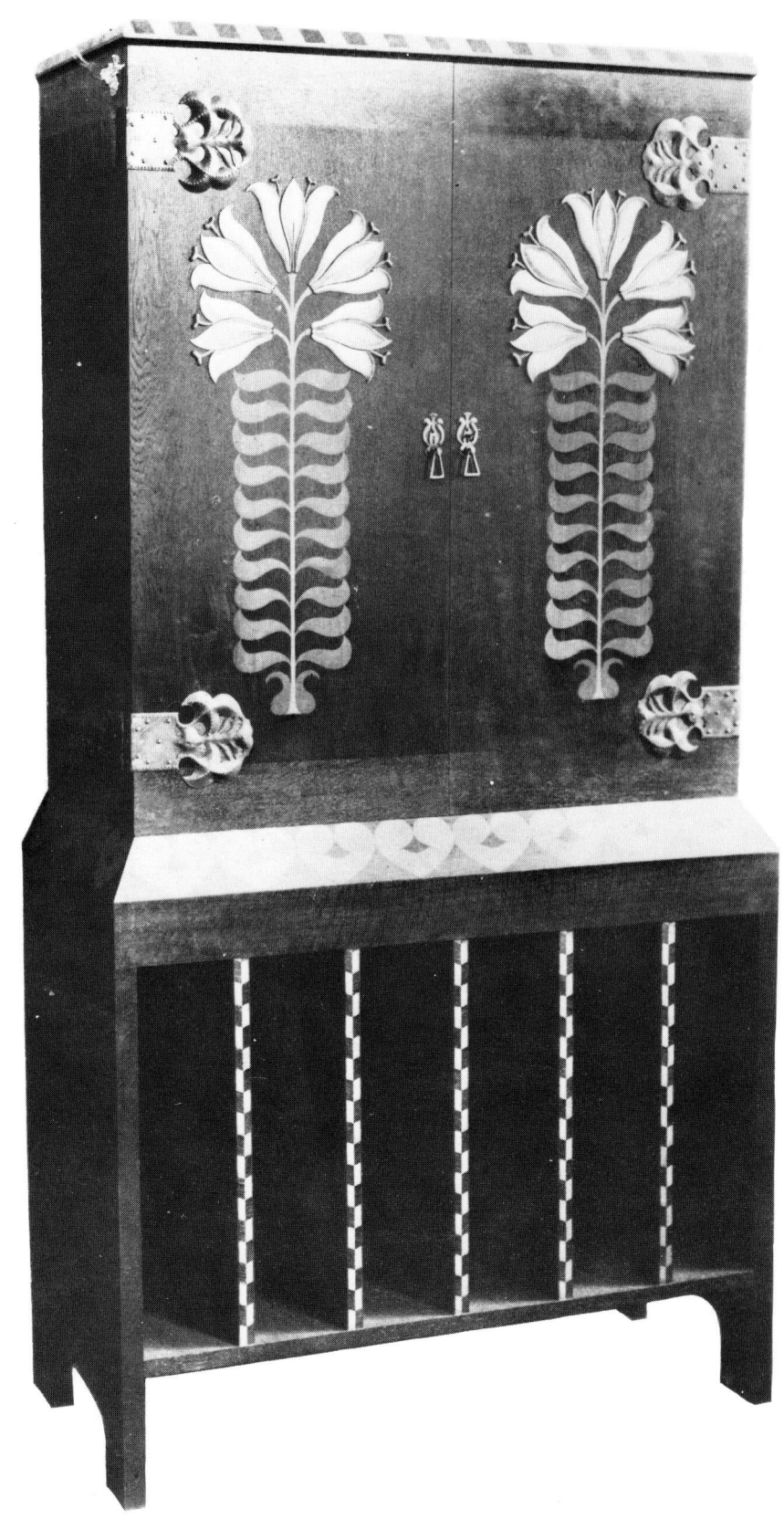

3 THE ESTABLISHMENT OF THE GUILDS

Ruskin's abortive Guild of St. George had indicated the way in which a democratic artistic community might be set up and the framework by which the individual, by sublimating his will to the good of the whole, gains true freedom of expression. The parallel with the protective idea of the Trade Unions is inescapable, though the community which C. R. Ashbee set up at Chipping Campden was, in practice, more like a religious one, with its communal meeting rooms, and the rehabilitation work on the village houses undertaken by all the members of the small society for the common weal. The rumblings of socialism implicit in the idea of a guild, which had been faint enough for Ruskin to ignore, now rose to a crescendo.

Ashbee's Guild of Handicraft was based on socialist principles, and it was hardly the fault of the founder if the universal happiness which he had envisaged did not materialise. Batchelder noted, on a visit to Chipping Campden in 1905, that 'Co-operation that does not co-operate breeds discontent in those who are co-operated upon'.[1] Ruskin's Guild of St. George was doomed because his personality was inimical, in its paternalism, to the concept of co-operation. Both Morris and Ashbee had a paternalistic side to their characters, which they were at considerable pains to suppress.

Even so, their creations, either Company or Guild, remain distinctively their own, and even Ashbee's careful insistence on the recognition of the separate contributions of his individual craftsmen has never made the Guild of Handicraft one whit less his personal monument. In retrospect the guilds can be seen to have been aesthetic in their conception as much as in their influence, but it remained a source of disappointment to committed socialists like Morris and Ashbee that the guilds were unable to provide art for the people.

125 M.H. Baillie Scott – Decorated and inlaid cabinet made by C.R. Ashbee for the Grand Duke of Hesse, 1898.

1 Andersen, Moore and Winter *California Design: 1910*, p. 16.

THE GUILD OF ST. GEORGE

British experimental co-operative
The Guild of St. George was set up by John Ruskin in 1871, and its foundation was announced in Letter VIII of *Fors Clavigera*, which appeared at the beginning of August in that year. Ruskin himself was to be the Master, contributing to the

finances of the Guild one tenth of his possessions. The St. George's fund was launched with a gift of £7,000 from Ruskin, but only £236 was collected from the public over the next three years, thus indicating their indifference to the grandiose programme set out for the Guild by its founder. This included nothing less than the reformation of the existing social system and the destruction of the industrial society which was to be replaced by the mediaeval system of masters and servants, artists and artisans with a common interest in the quality of life and work.

Well ahead of his time in his ideas for fighting industrial pollution, and far behind it in his paternalistic attitude to the potential Guildsmen, Ruskin's achievements were inevitably disappointing; a small cottage museum near Sheffield, some 'ideal' workmen's dwellings in Wales (reminding one of Prince Albert and his workingmen's cottages) and some land which was never effectively worked, were all that the elaborate planning and dreaming produced. However, the seeds were sown that were to produce the sub-structure of Guilds and Societies which under-pinned the Arts and Crafts Movement.

ARTHUR HEYGATE MACKMURDO (1851–1942)

British architect and designer

Mackmurdo was apprenticed to T. Chatfield Clarke before becoming a pupil of James Brooks in 1869. In 1873 he attended Ruskin's lectures delivered in Ruskin's capacity as Slade Professor at Oxford, and in the following year travelled in Italy with him. In 1875 Mackmurdo set up his own practice at 28 Southampton Street in London. He made two further trips to Italy in 1878 and 1880 where he filled his notebooks with architectural sketches as well as extensive studies of vegetation and other nature notes. He met William Morris when he was twenty-six, and this contact aroused his interest in the applied arts which he was later to practise so successfully. In 1882 he set up the Century Guild which aimed to produce decorative work in every branch of interior design and 'to render all branches of art the sphere no longer of the tradesman but of the artist'.

The first issue of *The Hobby Horse* appeared in 1884, published by Ruskin's protégé, George Allen, who had printed the extraordinary *Fors Clavigera* open letters 'to the workmen and labourers of Great Britain' — read eagerly by Mackmurdo as they appeared. Mackmurdo's architectural work included the Savoy Hotel (1889) and a house in Chelsea for the artist Mortimer Menpes (1899). In 1900 he went to live in Essex, and in 1904 started building his own house, Great Ruffins. In his old age he abandoned architecture in order to devote himself to the development of his theories on currency reform.

126 A.H. Mackmurdo – Mahogany chair with carved and inlaid decoration made by E. Goodhall for the Century Guild stand at the Liverpool International Exhibition in 1886.

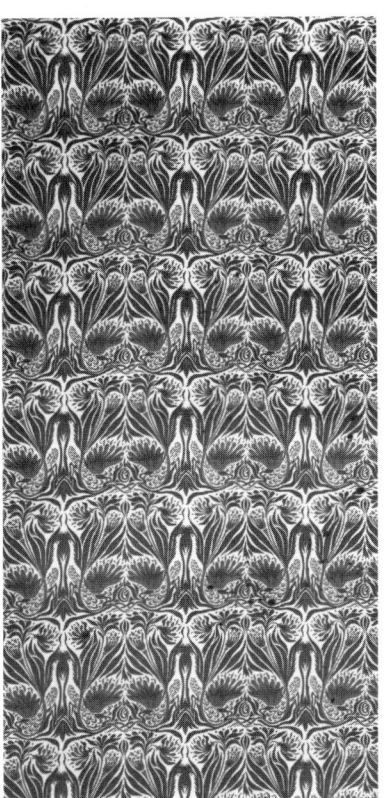

127 A.H. Mackmurdo – 'Peacock'. Printed cotton designed for the Century Guild, 1883.

THE CENTURY GUILD

British Craft Guild

The Century Guild was formed in 1882 by A. H. Mackmurdo and Selwyn Image, and included Herbert P. Horne, Benjamin Creswick the sculptor, Clement Heaton, metalworker, enamellist and stained glass designer, and George Esling and Kellock Brown, both metalworkers. Heywood Sumner, the designer who became Master of the Art Workers' Guild in 1894 and William De Morgan were also associated with the Century Guild. The Guild carried out decorative work of all kinds, much of it to Mackmurdo's design, but — true to the spirit of the Guild ideal — the work was presented as a co-operative effort, and it is often hard to disentangle individual attributions in their productions unless the pieces are signed. The Guild members designed and furnished a complete Music Room which was first shown at the Health Exhibition in London in 1884, and subsequently, with minor additions and alterations, at the Inventions Exhibition in 1887.

In 1884 *The Hobby Horse*, the Guild magazine, was started. It was printed at the Chiswick Press, and lavishly illustrated with woodcut decorations by Selwyn Image and Herbert Horne. After the first issue the magazine did not appear again until 1886 when it was jointly edited by Image and Horne. In 1893 Horne took over the sole editorship and changed both the distinctive cover and the format.

The Guild flourished until 1888, but from then on little work was undertaken by the Guild as such although the members continued to work in close association. Though relatively short-lived, the Guild exerted a considerable influence on the Craft revival movement. With the exception of Ruskin's ill-fated St. George's Guild, it was the first of the craft guilds to be set up, and in this respect can be seen as profoundly influential on the shape and scope of the movement and, in addition, Mackmurdo's ideas on design were widely copied. The design for the title page of his *Wren's City Churches* is regarded as the first, and one of the most important documents of Art Nouveau inspiration, and the stands, both for the Century Guild and for Cope's tobacco company which were shown at the Liverpool Exhibition, were the source of many of the distinctive decorative features in interior design of the turn of the century.

SELWYN IMAGE (1849–1930)

British designer and illustrator

After graduating from Oxford (where he had met Ruskin), in 1872, Image became a curate at Tottenham, moving to St. Anne's, Soho in 1876, while continuing to design at the same time. He was dismissed from his curacy in 1882 and in the same year he joined A. H. Mackmurdo in founding the Century

Guild. As well as executing the title page for *The Hobby Horse*, (a quarterly magazine issued by the Century Guild) he produced a number of other graphic works, designed mosaics and stained glass for Mortahoe Church in Devon, and embroideries for the Royal School of Needlework. He became Master of the Art Workers' Guild in 1900, and Slade Professor of Fine Arts at Oxford from 1910 to 1916.

HERBERT PERCY HORNE (1864–1916)

British designer, writer and antiquarian
Born in Chelsea, Herbert Horne entered the office of Robert Vigers of Old Jewry in 1880 to train as a surveyor. In 1882 he became a part-time pupil of architectural drawing and design with A. H. Mackmurdo, joining him full-time a year later, having given up surveying. He designed textiles, metalwork and wallpapers for the Century Guild and decorations for *The Hobby Horse*, which he had helped Mackmurdo to produce in 1884. In 1885 he entered into partnership with Mackmurdo, and designed the Chapel of Rest in the Bayswater Road in 1889 (destroyed 1940). In 1890 the partnership was dissolved, and he devoted himself to writing. In 1900 he retired to Florence where he spent the next seven years writing a life of Botticelli. He bought the Palazzo Fossi in 1915 and bequeathed it with the contents in the form of his art collection of furniture, ceramics, drawings and pictures to the City of Florence. It was re-named the Museo Horne.

ART WORKERS' GUILD & THE ARTS AND CRAFTS EXHIBITION SOCIETY

The Art Workers' Guild was founded in London in 1884 by the members of the St. George's Art Society, a group of artists and architects who were pupils or assistants in the office of Richard Norman Shaw, and is still in existence today. The dominant five in the St. George's Art Society were W. R. Lethaby, Ernest Newton, Edward Prior, Mervyn Macartney and Gerald Horsley, all prominent Arts and Crafts architects, and all founder members of the Art Workers' Guild. They were joined early on by the members of another group known as 'The Fifteen', led by Lewis F. Day and Walter Crane. Nearly all the artists, architects, craftsmen and designers of any importance to the Craft Revival Movement were members of the Art Workers' Guild, which provided a valuable focus of public attention, a meeting place for discussion and a platform for lectures on techniques and styles. The roll-call of the early members includes such distinguished names as J. D. Sedding,

128 Lewis F. Day – Tile panel designed for the Pilkington Tile and Pottery Co., *c*. 1902.

Basil Champneys, Beresford Pite, C. F. A. Voysey, Harrison Townsend, A. H. Mackmurdo, William Morris, C. R. Ashbee, Richard Norman Shaw, George Walton, Edwin Lutyens and Roger Fry.

The Arts and Crafts Exhibition Society developed as an extension of the Guild's activities, being set up in 1888 by a splinter group from the Guild who felt that Guild-sponsored exhibitions were a necessary part of the Guild programme. Exhibitions were held in 1888, 1889 and 1890, but the quality of the exhibits had declined noticeably by the time the third exhibition took place and it was decided to limit them to tri-annual events in the future. Thereafter the Society held exhibitions every three years until the outbreak of the First World War, providing an invaluable showcase for the Craft Movement designers. It is possible to trace the development of the Craft Revival style through the reports of the exhibitions which appeared in contemporary periodicals, notably *The Studio* and the *Art Journal*.

The early exhibitions were enlivened by lectures and demonstrations — for example, in 1888, by William Morris talking on tapestry weaving, George Simmonds on modelling and sculpture, Emery Walker on printing, Cobden-Sanderson on book-binding and Walter Crane on design (see *Arts and Crafts Essays* in bibliography). Branches were established in other parts of the country, and undoubtedly the Guild, with the Exhibition Society, provided the cohesion which ensured the long survival of the Craft Movement in England and its lingering influence, which is discernable even today.

AMERICAN ART WORKERS' GUILD

The American Art Workers' Guild was founded about 1885 in Providence, Rhode Island, by Sidney Richmond Burleigh (1853–1931), artist and designer, Charles Walter Stetson (1858–1911), painter, and industrialist John Aldrich. The Guild members designed buildings, designed and made silver-ware and also other metalwork. Furniture decorated with panel paintings was another speciality of the group. Their most ambitious project was the Fleur de Lys studio building in Providence which was undertaken in 1885. The furniture is in a style reminiscent of Morris, but without the Pre-Raphaelite refinement.

WALTER CRANE (1845–1915)

British book illustrator, designer and painter
Second son of the portrait painter Thomas Crane, Walter Crane showed a precocious talent for drawing, and his father supervised his early efforts as well as teaching him the rudiments of method. Almost without formal education, he

129 Walter Crane – Design for a ceiling paper, 'La Margarete', for Jeffrey and Co., 1877.

was apprenticed at the age of thirteen to the wood-engraver, William James Linton. When his apprenticeshp was over he undertook a number of routine and ill-paid commisions before making his name as a nursery-book illustrator with the Toy books, the first of which appeared in 1865. He is probably best-known in this capacity for his *Baby's Opera* which appeared in 1877, and it was through these books that his name became linked with those of Randolph Caldecott and Kate Greenaway, making up the famous triumvirate of Victorian children's illustrators.

He exhibited at the Royal Academy for the first time in 1862 at the age of seventeen, but after this his work was only accepted once more ten years later. He showed mainly at the Dudley Gallery, at Sir Lindsay Coutts' Grosvenor Gallery and regularly with the Arts and Crafts Exhibition Society after its foundation in 1888. He designed wallpapers for Jeffery and Co. from 1874, the first one called 'the Queen of Hearts' being issued in 1875, and he had produced over fifty designs by 1912. He also designed fabrics for various manufacturers, including Wardle and Co. and Edmund Potter and Co., one tapestry for Morris and Co. and two carpets for Templeton's. His ceramic designs included vases and jugs for Wedgwood, sets of tiles based on the illustrations to the Toy books, as well as the 'Seasons' and the 'Times of Day' for Maw and Company, for whom he also designed vases, jugs and dishes, plates for Mintons, and tiles and large ornamental dishes for Pilkington's Tile and Pottery Co. Other decorative works included ornamental plasterwork, mosaics and designs for stained glass.

Crane's association with Morris led to his becoming interested in the Socialist League which he joined in 1883, an interest fostered in his boyhood by his master, W. J. Linton. In 1882 he had begun attending the meetings of 'The Fifteen', a group which included Lewis F. Day and Henry Holiday. In 1884 they joined with the members of the St. George's Art Society, all of them pupils and assistants of the architect Norman Shaw, to found the Art Workers' Guild, Crane himself becoming the Master of the Guild in 1888. He also became President of the Arts and Crafts Exhibition Society in 1888, and remained in this position, with the exception of the period 1893–1896 when Morris was President, until 1912. He became Director of Design at Manchester Municipal College in 1893 and Principal of the Royal College of Art at South Kensington in 1898. From his lectures evolved his books on art teaching, *The Bases of Design* (1898) and *Line and Form* (1900).

In 1902 he organised a display of British Arts and Crafts for the Exhibition at Turin, and in 1905 he received the Gold Medal of the Royal Society of Arts. He died a few months after his wife in 1915.

130 C.R. Ashbee – Silver mounted green glass decanter, made by the Guild of Handicraft, 1901.

131

132

LEWIS FOREMAN DAY (1845–1910)

British designer and writer

Lewis F. Day was born in Peckham Rye on the outskirts of London of a Quaker family and was educated in France and Germany. In 1865 he became a clerk in the works of Lavers and Barraud, glass painters, subsequently moving to Clayton and Bell as a designer of stained glass, and while with them in 1870 he worked on the decorations of Eaton Hall in Cheshire. Later in the same year he started his own business designing textiles, wallpapers, stained glass, embroidery, carpets, tiles, pottery and book-covers for various manufacturers including Ward and Co., Jeffery and Co., Howell and James, Maw and Co., and Pilkington's Tile and Pottery Co. He gathered together a group of artists interested in design, meeting to discuss the relationship of art and design with everyday life. Known as 'The Fifteen' they joined with the pupils and assistants of Norman Shaw to form the Art Workers' Guild (1884) of which L. F. Day was later Master, and the Arts and Crafts Exhibition Society, (1888). As well as lecturing, examining and teaching, L. F. Day was the author of numerous widely influential books on pattern-making, ornament and design, and a regular contributor to the *Art Journal* and the *Magazine of Art*.

PILKINGTON TILE AND POTTERY CO. LTD

Glass and pottery manufacturers

The long-established Pilkington's Glassworks set up their pottery in 1897 with William Burton, who had been a chemist with Wedgwood's, as technical and artistic director. The firm specialised in glaze effects and in the production of tiles designed for them by Walter Crane, Lewis F. Day and C. F. A. Voysey. After the turn of the century they added production of lustre-ware, given the trade-name of Royal Lancastrian. The decoration was carried out by a number of accomplished ceramic painters, including Gordon M. Forsyth, Richard Joyce, Charles E. Cundall, Gwladys Rogers and William S. Mycock. In the twenties matt glazes were developed and added to the production of the firm.

KESWICK SCHOOL OF INDUSTRIAL ART

British craft and metalworking class

The Keswick School was founded as an evening institute by Canon and Mrs Rawnsley in 1884 at Keswick in Cumberland. It was expanded to include daytime classes in 1898. Harold Stabler and Herbert J. Maryon, the metalworker and jeweller, were both full-time directors and designers connected with the school, and the products of the classes reflect their influence in the simple structural shapes and minimal ornament. Keswick

131 C.R. Ashbee – Loop-handled covered bowl in silver with enamelled decoration, made by the Guild of Handicraft, 1905.

132 R.L.B. Rathbone – Beaten copper candlesticks decorated with bands of punched floral ornaments, 1902.

metalwork and jewellery was sold through the Home Arts and Industries Association, and the venture was similar in scope and achievement to the Yattendon Metalworking class which was organised by Mrs Waterhouse.

R. LLEWELLYN RATHBONE (1864–1939)

British designer and metalworker
Rathbone was a cousin of Harold Rathbone, the head of the Della Robbia Pottery and a relation of W. A. S. Benson, who possibly influenced him in his choice of metalworking as a career. He worked on projects with Mackmurdo, Heywood Sumner and C. F. A. Voysey producing metal fittings and utensils. He set up a workshop in Liverpool, and also taught in the metalworking class at the University there from about 1898 until 1903. He later came to London where he was first head of the Art School of the Sir John Cass Technical Institute, and taught at the London County Council Central School of Arts and Crafts. He made a small amount of jewellery and published two books on the subject, namely *Simple Jewellery* in 1910 which was followed by *Unit Jewellery* in 1920. After he came to London he interested himself increasingly in the production of unit metalwork, largely abandoning the more elaborate work of his Liverpool days.

HAROLD STABLER (1872–1945)

British artist, craftsman potter, silversmith and enamellist
Stabler studied woodwork and stone-carving at the Kendal School of Art. He became Head of Canon and Mrs Rawnsley's Keswick School of Industrial Art in about 1898, but left after a short time to join R. Llewellyn Rathbone in the metalworking department at the Liverpool University Art School in 1899. He came to London with Rathbone and taught with him at the Sir John Cass Technical Institute in about 1906, and succeeded Rathbone as Head of the Institute's Art School between 1907 and 1937. With his wife Phoebe he designed and executed a number of pottery figures. Some of these were subsequently produced in editions by the Carter, Stabler, Adams pottery, of which he was a co-founder. He was associated for a period with the Poole Pottery. He was also a founding member of the Design and Industries Association in 1915, thus arriving with a number of his fellow craft-revivalists at the point of departure which had been envisaged by Sir Henry Cole and Prince Albert over half a century earlier.

DELLA ROBBIA CO. LTD.

British art pottery company
Della Robbia was established at Birkenhead in 1894 by Conrad Dressler, the sculptor, and Harold Rathbone, a painter and

133 Edgar Wood – Cupboard with metalwork by George Wragge, illustrated in *The Studio*, Vol. 15, 1898, p.285.

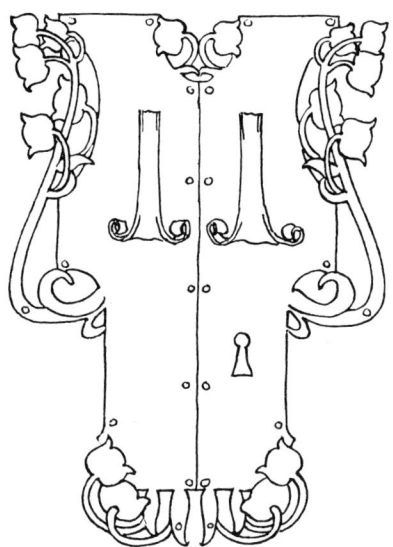

134 George Wragge – Metal furniture fitting used by Edgar Wood for his furniture, illustrated in *The Studio*, Vol. 14, 1898.

pupil of Ford Madox Brown, with the intention of concentrating on the production of architectural embellishments. Hollow-wares were also made from an early date, and painted sgraffito decoration was a characteristic of the firm's work. The name of the firm was intended to suggest an aesthetic allegiance to the Italian Renaissance, not to imply the use of similar techniques or the revival of sculptural style for which the original Della Robbia was famous, though low relief plaques after designs by Robert Anning Bell were made by the pottery. Most of the modellers and decorators were recruited from local art schools, but the Italian Carlo Manzoni came to them from the Granville Pottery, Hanley in about 1897. The commercial management of the firm was on an insufficiently solid basis and in 1906 it was closed down.

EDGAR WOOD (1860–1935)

British architect and designer

Edgar Wood was born near Manchester in the cotton spinning town of Middleton, of a well-to-do, middle class family connected with the cotton trade. Wood's early ambition was to be an artist but his father wished him to join the family cotton business, and the profession of architect was thus chosen as a compromise solution to these differing aims. Wood was articled to the Manchester firm of Mills and Murgatroyd and he qualified in 1885, immediately setting up in practice independently. By 1893 he was enjoying substantial success with an office in Manchester and subsidiary offices in his home town, Middleton, and another local town, Oldham.

His speciality was working in the vernacular style of his home region, the Pennine foothills, in the best Arts and Crafts tradition. In 1904 he entered into partnership with Henry Sellers, a native of Oldham, and a year junior to him in age. In 1910 a legacy made Wood financially independent and he began to spend less time on his architectural work and more on painting, realising at last the frustrated ambitions of his youth. In 1922 he retired to Italy to devote himself to art.

CHARLES FRANCIS ANNESLEY VOYSEY (1857–1941)

British architect, designer and typographer

Born at Hessle, near Kingston-upon-Hull, and educated at Dulwich College, Charles Francis Annesley was the son of the Rev. Charles Voysey, founder of the Theistic Church, who was removed from the Church of England for preaching against the doctrine of hell-fire. From 1874 to 1880 Voysey worked as a pupil in the office of J. P. Seddon, then briefly as an assistant to George Devey. In 1882 he set up his own office, but concentrated at first on decorative work rather than architecture, selling his first designs for fabrics and wallpaper in 1883. In 1884 he joined the Art Workers' Guild, and his first house was not built until 1888.

In 1891 Voysey designed a house in Bedford Park. Known as the 'Grey House' it stands out from its neighbours, by this time fifteen years old and in a style which was rapidly being superseded, as a foretaste of Voysey's more uncompromising style, soon to supplant the Shavian 'Queen Anne' as the most potent influence on urban and suburban development. In 1900 he completed his own house, 'The Orchard' at Chorley Wood in Hertfordshire, for which he designed much of the furniture, the decoration and the fittings. His characteristic style, simple, linear, and with almost no surface decoration, was to be widely copied in the 'artistic' interiors of the period.

In 1915 he became chief designer to the Liquor Control Board, and in 1924 Master of the Art Workers' Guild. Voysey's work was known on the continent through his participation in a number of exhibitions held abroad; he showed architectural work in the Salons de la Libre Esthetique in 1894 and 1897, and he also exhibited alongside the Glasgow School 'Four' at Liège in 1895 and in Turin in 1902. Writing in 1931, ten years before Voysey's death, John Betjeman quotes Fra Newbery, the head of the Glasgow School of Art, as saying that Mackintosh derived his inspiration from Voysey who was just setting up in practice at the outset of Mackintosh's training. In 1931 an exhibition covering all aspects of Voysey's varied artistic career was mounted at the Batsford Gallery under the auspices of the Architectural Review, and among the work shown there was little that would seem out of place in an exhibition of the most daring contemporary work.

135 C.F.A. Voysey – Oak chair with padded leather back and seat designed for the Essex and Suffolk Insurance Co., 1909.

137 M.H. Baillie Scott – Writing cabinet, designed for the Grand Duke of Hesse's palace in Darmstadt, 1898, made by the Guild of Handicraft. From a photograph in one of C.R. Ashbee's albums.

CHARLES ROBERT ASHBEE
(1863–1942)

British architect, designer, silversmith and jeweller
Charles Robert Ashbee was born in Isleworth and educated at Wellington and King's College, Cambridge. He was articled to G. F. Bodley between 1883 and 1885, and lived at the pioneer University Settlement at Toynbee Hall in the East End of London. Here he started a Ruskin reading class which developed into an art class. In 1887 with some of his evening class students he undertook the decoration of the Toynbee Hall dining-room. This group became the nucleus of the School of Handicraft, which was started in the same year, and the Guild of Handicraft (1888), which had Ashbee himself as chief designer, three foundation members and a capital of £50. The Guild is now chiefly known and admired for the metalwork and jewellery designed by Ashbee, and for the furniture and metalwork made for the Grand Duke of Hesse in the workshops at Essex House, where Ashbee also established the printing press used by Morris at Kelmscott House.

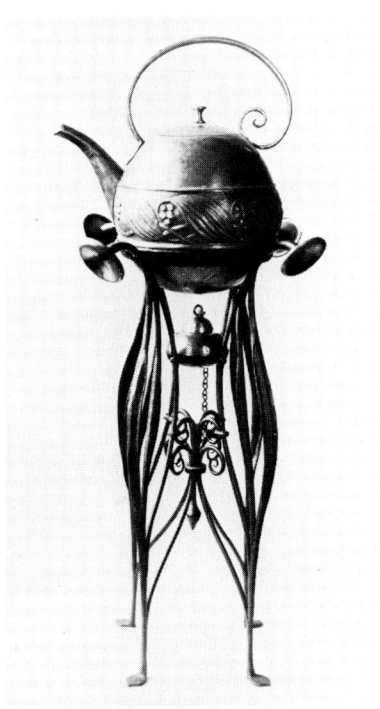

136 C.R. Ashbee – Kettle and stand, from a photograph in one of Ashbee's albums.

In 1890 Ashbee acquired for the Guild the lease of Essex House, a Georgian mansion in the Mile End Road. Retail premises were opened at 16a Brook Street, and these were retained when the Guild moved to Chipping Campden in Gloucestershire in 1902. Here an ambitious programme of re-habilitation was undertaken, transforming the village of Chipping Campden into a community of Guild workers and their families. The expenses incurred by the Guild in Gloucestershire and in retaining the retail premises in London far outran their receipts from the Guild products and in 1907 they were forced into voluntary liquidation. Many of the workers continued to work independently, some still using Ashbee's designs.

Ashbee himself took up his neglected architectural practice again. His architectural work, like that of Voysey, makes a genuine and relatively early attempt to break away from the historicism of his immediate predecessors. His own house, the 'Magpie and Stump' in Cheyne Walk was completed in 1895, and it is interesting to note that the taste for eclecticism which he displayed in the interior decorations and the furnishings is close to the taste of the 1970s, an indication of the extent to which Ashbee had managed to get away from the lingering High Victorianism of much contemporary design.

MACKAY HUGH BAILLIE SCOTT (1865–1945)

British architect and designer

M. H. Baillie Scott was born in Kent, eldest of the fourteen children of a Scottish Laird, owner of a valuable sheep-farm in Australia. Baillie Scott attended the Royal Agricultural College at Cirencester with the intention of making his career in managing the Australian sheep farm. He had shown an interest in drawing and painting since childhood, and on completing his training at Cirencester in 1885 he abandoned the idea of going to Australia and decided instead to become an architect. In 1886 he was articled to Major Charles Davis, City Architect of Bath. In 1889 Baillie Scott married and went with his bride Florence (née Nash) to Douglas on the Isle of Man, where he set up as an architect, working first from a flat for four years until his 'Red House', built to his own designs, was completed. When he first arrived in Douglas, Baillie Scott attended classes at the Isle of Man School of Art where he encountered Archibald Knox who was teaching there. The two men collaborated on the design and execution of stained glass, iron grates and copper fireplace hoods which were installed in the houses built by Baillie Scott on the island.

In 1897 Baillie Scott was commissioned by the Grand Duke of Hesse to redecorate and furnish the drawing-room and dining-room in the Ducal Palace at Darmstadt, which he did in collaboration with C. R. Ashbee. The furniture, light fixtures

138 M.H. Baillie Scott – Writing cabinet with doors open.

and metalwork were made under Ashbee's supervision in the workshops of the Guild of Handicraft. In 1901 Baillie Scott entered his 'House for an art lover' in the competition organised by the Zeitschrift fur Innendekoration, the competition to which C. R. Mackintosh also submitted a much-admired entry. The prize was not awarded outright as none of the entries came up to the exacting standards of the judges, but Baillie Scott's entry was awarded the highest prize which was given. At this same date Baillie Scott gave up his practice in Douglas, sold the 'Red House' and moved to Bedford, possibly to be within more convenient reach of John White for whom he had been designing furniture since about 1898.

By 1901 White was able to issue a catalogue of furniture made to Baillie Scott's designs at his Pyghtle Works which numbered at least 120 pieces. The furniture was sold through Liberty's, and probably through the showrooms at 134 New Bond Street which White acquired in the early years of the present century. In 1905 Baillie Scott employed A. Edgar Beresford (born 1881) as his assistant and in 1919 Beresford became his partner. In 1914 Baillie Scott left Bedford and the next few years were spent moving about from place to place, first in London, then in Surrey, Kent, Bath and back to Kent again. The practice was established in Gray's Inn Road. In 1939 Baillie Scott retired although Beresford carried on for a few more months. At the outbreak of the Second World War, however, he too gave up the practice with the intention of taking it up again later, but this, in fact, was not to be.

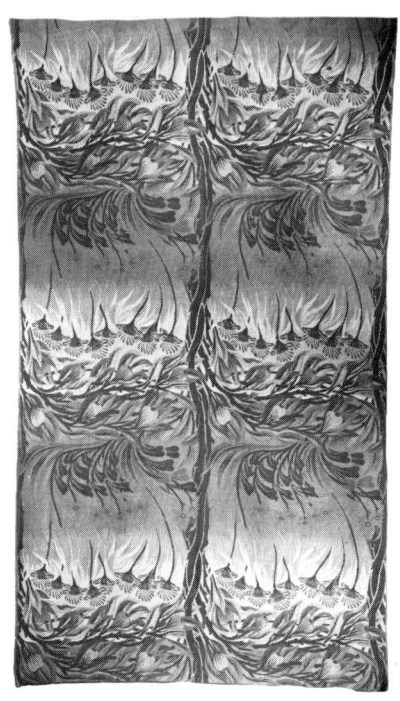

139

139 A.H. Mackmurdo – Woven hanging, *c*. 1882.

140 Herbert P. Horne – Pierced brass fender for the Century Guild, *c*. 1886.

140

141

142

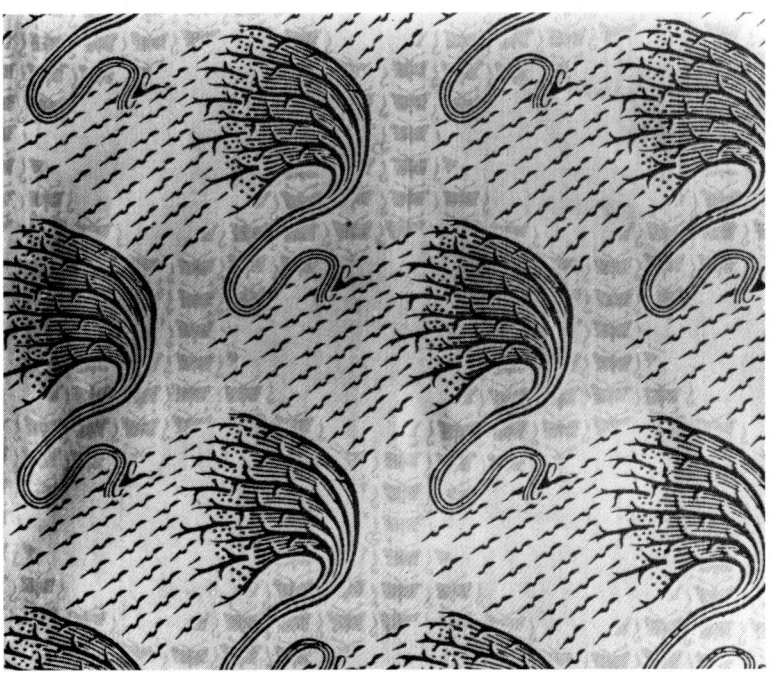

143

141 A.H. Mackmurdo – Dining chair for the Century Guild, 1882-83.

142 A.H. Mackmurdo – Oak desk for the Century Guild, c. 1885.

143 A.H. Mackmurdo – 'Thorns and Butterflies'. Cretonne designed for the Century Guild, c. 1886.

123

144

144 The Century Guild – Cabinet, detail of central fretted decorative bracket.

145 The Century Guild – Cabinet with shelf supported on fretted brackets, c. 1886.

146 A.H. Mackmurdo – 'Cromer Bird'. Printed cotton, designed c. 1884 and printed by Simpson and Godlee.

147 C.F.A. Voysey – 'Nympheas'. Printed cotton, c. 1898.

145

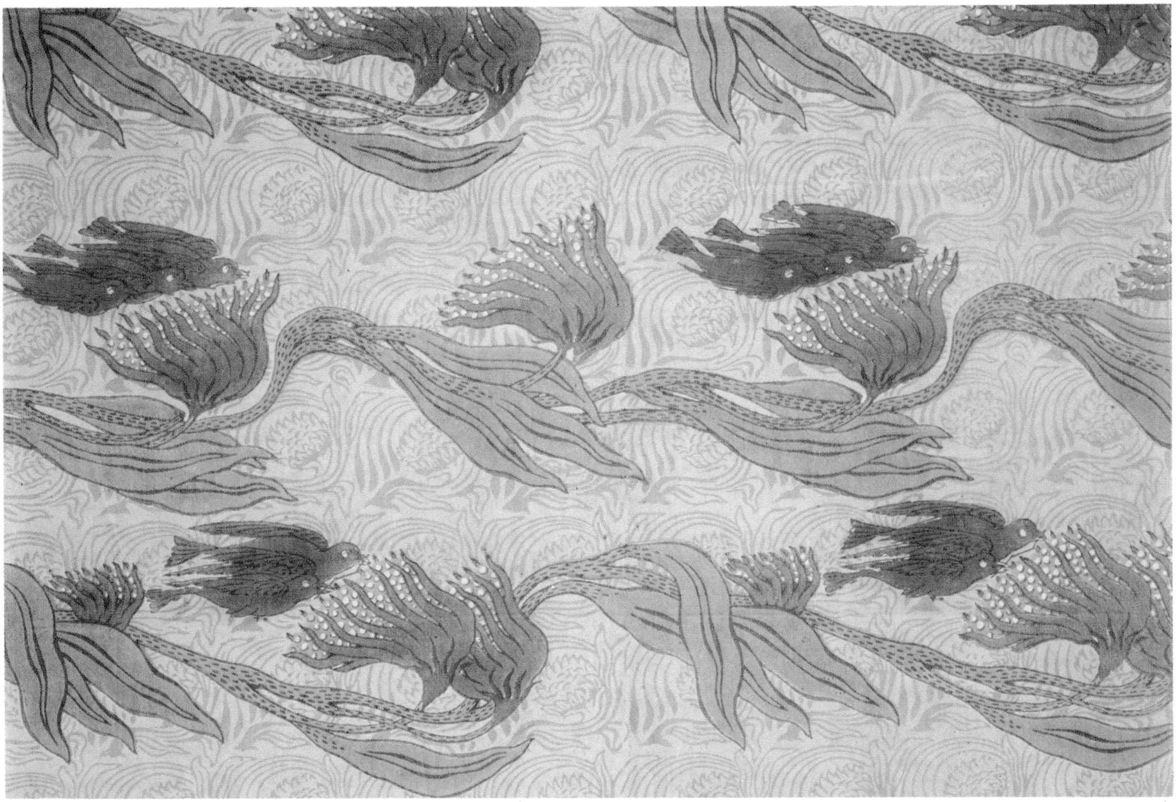

146

147

148

149

148 A.H. Mackmurdo – Mahogany settle, with cane insets, hangings and upholstery in the 'Tulip' chintz (1875), Century Guild, *c.* 1886.

149 C.F.A. Voysey – Detail of the door panel from an oak writing desk with brass hinges, made for W. Ward Higgs, 1896.

150 C.F.A. Voysey – The 'Kelmscott' Cabinet, oak, with hinges and decorative fittings in brass. Designed for W. Ward Higgs and made by F. Coote, 1899.

151

152

151 M.H. Baillie Scott – 'Manxman' piano, in ebonized wood with inset decoration of stylised leaves, flowers and fruit in pewter and coloured glass, made by John Broadwood and Sons, 1896.

152 C.R. Ashbee – Oak piano, with chevron banding and inset plaques in transluscent enamels, made by John Broadwood and Sons, c. 1898.

153

153 The Century Guild stand at the Liverpool Exhibition in 1886.

154 Herbert P. Horne – 'Angel with a trumpet'. Printed cotton, c. 1884.

155 The Century Guild – 'Leaf and Rose'. Printed velveteen, c. 1886.

154

155

157

156

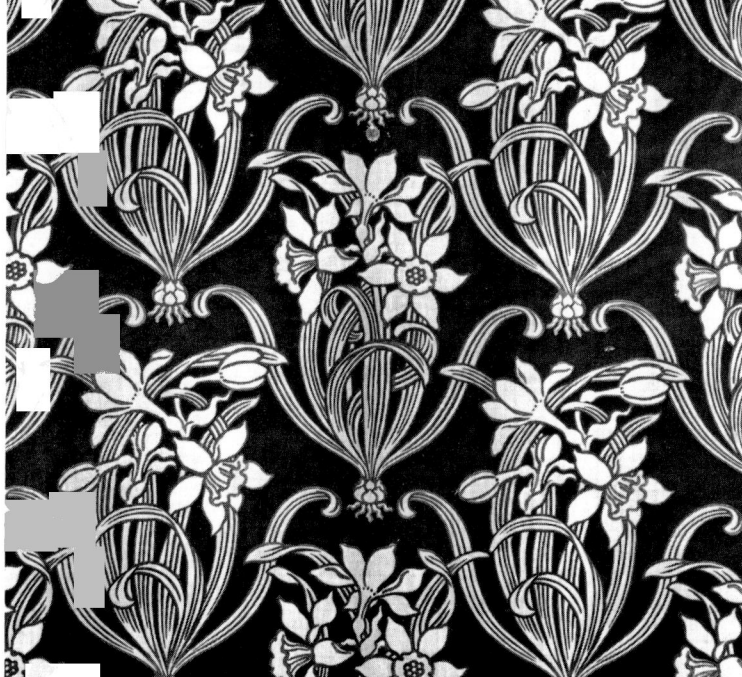

158

156 Walter Crane – Earthenware vase decorated in ruby lustre, made by Maw and Co., *c*. 1889.

157 Pilkington Tile and Pottery Co. – 'Lancastrian' two-handled cup, decorated with lustre and painted by Gordon M. Forsyth, 1908.

158 Lewis F. Day – 'Daffodils'. Printed velveteen, *c*. 1900.

159

160

159 Walter Crane – 'Cuenca' tile, designed for the Pilkington Tile and Pottery Co., *c*. 1902.

160 Walter Crane – 'Cuenca' tile, designed for the Pilkington Tile and Pottery Co., *c*. 1902.

161 Della Robbia Pottery Co. – Group of wares with painted and sgraffito decoration, *c*. 1890.

161

162 C.F.A. Voysey – Furniture mounts and handles, 1896-1905.

163 C.F.A. Voysey – Brass teapot, c. 1896.

164 C.F.A. Voysey – Painted wooden clock, 1896.

165 C.F.A. Voysey – Oak sideboard, c. 1900.

166 C.F.A. Voysey – Oak rush-seated chair, c. 1905.

167 C.F.A. Voysey – 'Bird and Leaf'. Silk and wool, designed for Alexander Norton, 1899.

168 C.F.A. Voysey – Printed linen, c. 1905.

165

166

167

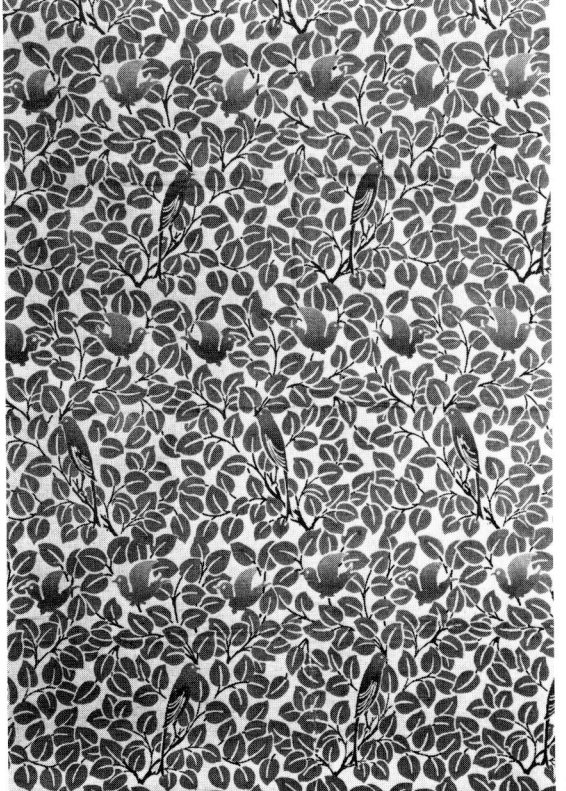

168

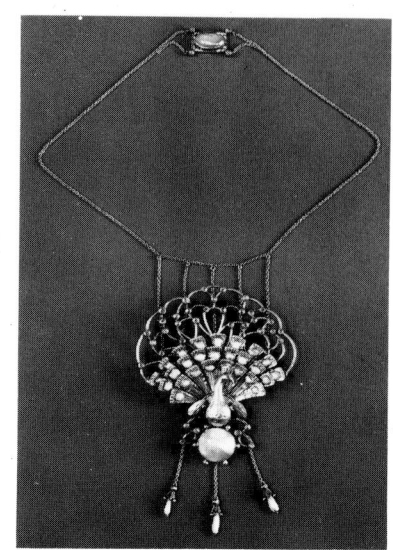

169 C.R. Ashbee – Silver bowl, designed for the Guild of Handicraft, c. 1893.

170 C.R. Ashbee – Pendant in silver, gold and baroque pearls, 1902.

171 C.R. Ashbee – Embossed silver tray with 'Peacock' design, 1896-97.

172

172 C.R. Ashbee – Silver mustard pot set with cabochon turquoises and with a glass liner, 1899-1900.

173 C.R. Ashbee – Silver bowl and cover, 1899-1900.

174 C.R. Ashbee – Examples of cutlery designed for the Guild of Handicraft, c. 1900.

173

174

175

176

177

175 Oak chair with ebony inlay and a rushed seat and back, possibly designed by E. Punnett. A version of this chair appears in a photograph of an Ashbee interior published in *The Studio*, made at High Wickham by William Birch, 1901.

176 M.H. Baillie Scott – Chair with inlaid and applied decoration, made by C.R. Ashbee's Guild of Handicraft for the palace of the Grand Duke of Hesse at Darmstadt, 1898.

177 C.R. Ashbee – Writing cabinet. A photograph from one of his scrapbooks.

178 M.H. Baillie Scott – Chair with embossed leather back designed for the Grand Duke of Hesse, made by the Guild of Handicraft. From a photograph in one of C.R. Ashbee's albums.

179 M.H. Baillie Scott – Settle designed for J.P. White's Pyghtle Works, 1901.

180 M.H. Baillie Scott – Writing cabinet designed for J.P. White's Pyghtle Works, 1901.

181 M.H. Baillie Scott – Chest and cupboard designed for J.P. White's Pyghtle Works, 1901.

178

179

180

181

182

4 'ART AND THE HANDICRAFTSMAN'

The American craft communities founded at this time, although avowedly based on Morris's ideals, did little towards establishing his socialism on a practical footing. They entertained no unreal hopes of alleviating the cultural lot of the masses, remaining hermetically sealed in their own escapist rural settings. In England the socialist ideals had inevitably been overriden by aesthetic considerations. Lip-service was paid to the original concept of art for all in the deliberate use of unpretentious materials — for instance it is rare to find valuable precious stones or gold used for craft jewellery, or exotic woods for the furniture — but within the limitations imposed by this discipline the craftsmen strove to produce the richest possible effect.

It is no coincidence that this new generation of artist-craftsmen were working for Edwardian patrons. For the first time in nearly a hundred years it was socially acceptable to be conspicuously rich and the ideals of a democratic art were paid scant consideration by such followers of the Arts and Crafts band-wagon as Ramsden and Carr, James Cromer Watt, Professor J. Hodel, J. Paul Cooper and a number of the Birmingham artists. Not only were many of these designers easily seduced into working for A. L. Liberty, but it is perhaps not without significance to recall that the most ambitious joint project undertaken by the Birmingham Group was the decoration of Madresfield Court for Lord and Lady Beauchamp, hardly an example of dedicated commitment to 'art for all'.

It had been proved and was finally recognised by the craftsmen that to produce art for the masses required mass-production, and it is significant to note how many of them, even the most idealistic, were to become members of the D.I.A. It is very doubtful whether the Home Arts and Industries exhibitions were extensively patronised by working class customers, and Morris was deeply disappointed to find that his patrons were invariably rich aesthetes. The craftsmen were thus able to devote their energies to the aesthetics of the craft revival movement, financed by those rich patrons who required that even their surroundings should demonstrate their adherence to the democratic principle.

182 J.D. Sedding – Design for the nave arcade of the Holy Trinity Church, Sloane Street, published in *The Builder*, October 1889.

JOHN DANDO SEDDING (1838–1891)

British architect and designer of metalwork, embroideries and wallpapers

Sedding was articled in 1858 to G. E. Street, in whose office he acquired his knowledge and understanding of Gothic architecture and ornament. The influence of this aspect of his own work was later to permeate the Arts and Crafts Movement through his pupils Henry Wilson and J. P. Cooper. In 1863 he left Street's office, and for the next two years concentrated mostly on decorative design. In 1865 he went into partnership with his brother Edmund, who was practising as an architect at Penzance in Cornwall. Three years later Edmund died, and J. D. Sedding moved to Bristol where he stayed until 1874, when he returned to London and set up as an architect and designer. In 1876 he met Ruskin and studied his views on observation and the use of natural forms as a basis for ornamental design, spending his holidays making detailed and careful studies of plants and foliage. In 1880 he was appointed diocesan architect of Bath and Wells.

In 1886 Sedding designed his revolutionary Church of the Holy Redeemer in Clerkenwell, in a severe classical style, a complete contrast to the richly decorated Holy Trinity in Sloane Street, the designs for which were begun a year earlier. In 1888 Sedding moved to West Wickham and only three years later he caught influenza and died. His practice was taken over by Henry Wilson, his chief assistant, who finished a number of outstanding commissions including many of the fittings and furnishings for Holy Trinity. This church was to be 'the most important church of London for observing the liberating effect of the Arts and Crafts movement on ecclesiastical architecture'.[1] It survives still, but may not last much longer against the threat of redevelopment. It was elaborately furnished and decorated in a mixture of flamboyant French Gothic and English perpendicular, with the help of — among others — Edward Burne-Jones, William Morris, Christopher Whall, the glass artist, F. W. Pomeroy, Henry Bates, Onslow Ford, Hamo Thornycroft and Alfred Gilbert, all sculptors, and Henry Wilson and Nelson Dawson, both metalworkers.

HENRY WILSON (1864–1934)

British architect, sculptor, jeweller and metalworker

Wilson studied architecture under John Oldrich Scott and John Belcher R.A. He became chief assistant to J. D. Sedding, and completed some projects left unfinished at the time of Sedding's death in 1891. Wilson's interest in metalwork dates from about 1890 and it gradually came to dominate his work. He set up his own metalworking shop in about 1895, and entered into a brief and unsuccessful partnership with Alexander Fisher (q.v.) a few years later. A pupil of Sedding's,

183 J.D. Sedding – Holy Trinity Church, Sloane Street, London, 1889.

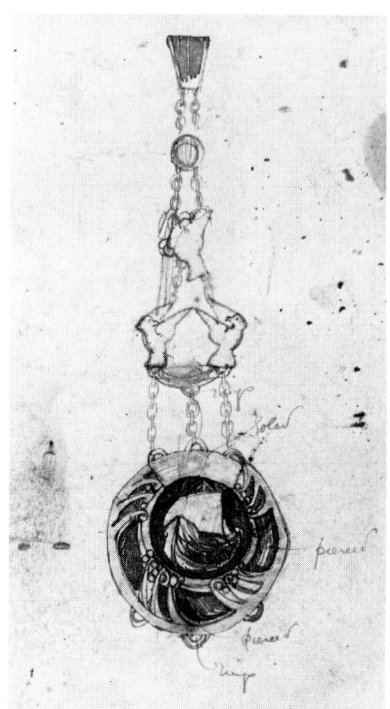

184 Henry Wilson – Design for a pendant, *c.* 1900.

---

1 Nicholas Pevsner *The Buildings of England, London*, Vol. II, p. 42, London 1952.

J. Paul Cooper (q.v.), studied jewellery and silverwork under one of Wilson's workshop assistants, and was profoundly influenced by Wilson's jewellery style. Their work is sometimes so close in style as to be virtually indistinguishable.

Wilson taught at the Central School of Arts and Crafts from 1896 and at the Royal College of Art from 1901. He joined the Art Workers' Guild in 1892 and became Master in 1917, and selected the English jewellery for the Paris Exhibitions in 1914 and 1925 (see chronology). He designed the bronze doors for the Anglican Cathedral of St. John the Divine in New York in about 1905. In 1903 he published *Silverwork and Jewellery*, which is still widely regarded as the best practical manual on the subject.

J. PAUL COOPER (1869–1933)

British architect, designer, goldsmith, silversmith and jeweller
Born in London, J. Paul Cooper was the son of a prosperous senior partner in a Leicester Hosiery works. He was educated at Bradfield College, and entered the office of J. D. Sedding in 1889 on the advice of W. R. Lethaby. Here he came under the influence of Henry Wilson, Sedding's chief assistant. Wilson took over the practice after Sedding's untimely death in 1891, and Cooper continued in the office assisting Wilson with the architectural work for the Duke of Portland. He began to take an interest in decorative art, including gesso-work, embroidery and silverwork in 1892. In 1900 he began to take lessons in jewellery from Wilson's chief assistant at his workshop in Vicarage Gate. Late in 1901 he took up his appointment as head of the Metalwork Department at the Birmingham School of Art but in 1906 he gave up the job in order to devote the rest of his life to craft-work.

During his career (i.e. from 1892–1933) J. Paul Cooper made nearly fourteen hundred pieces of jewellery, silverwork, gesso-work and other metalwork, all of which are meticulously recorded in his stock books, and so he must be regarded as one of the most important of the Arts and Crafts artists in these fields. His craft-work entirely dominated his working life and, apart from designing his own house, his architectural career was entirely abandoned after 1898, unlike Wilson, Ashbee or Mackmurdo, whose craft output was necessarily much more limited. In 1914 he exhibited 84 pieces at the Exposition de l'Art Décoratif in Paris and in 1931 an important retrospective exhibition of his work was held at Walker's Galleries in London. He died at the comparatively early age of sixty-three and his unfinished commissions were completed by his son Francis who followed in his father's footsteps as a silversmith, and who still runs his father's workshop in the house at Westerham which J. P. Cooper designed in 1910 — an almost unaltered example of Arts and Crafts architecture, every detail carefully designed by Cooper and his friends.

185 J. Paul Cooper – Pendant, silver and gold set with precious and semi-precious stones.

NELSON DAWSON (1859–1942)

British painter, silversmith and jeweller

Nelson Dawson trained as an architect, then studied painting at the South Kensington Schools. In 1881 he took up metalworking. He studied enamelling under Alexander Fisher and, after his marriage in 1893, set up a workshop with his wife Edith Robinson whom he taught enamelling and who subsequently carried out the enamelled decoration which is a characteristic feature of much of his work. In 1901 he set up the Artificers' Guild (q.v.) in his Chiswick workshop, but it passed into the possession of Montague Fordham in 1903. Nelson Dawson gave up metalworking in 1914 and devoted the rest of his life to painting.

ARTIFICERS' GUILD

The Artificers' Guild was founded in 1901 by Nelson Dawson (q.v.) with one of his workshop employees, Edward Spencer, as a fellow-guildsman. It was acquired by Montague Fordham, one-time director of the Birmingham Guild of Handicraft (q.v.) in 1903, and was subsequently installed in the Fordham Gallery in Maddox Street, where work was already available from Henry Wilson (q.v.) and May Morris (q.v.). J. Paul Cooper (q.v.) executed a large number of works for the Gallery and the Artificers' Guild style could be said to derive from him through his influence on Edward Spencer. The Guild moved to premises at 4 Conduit Street after the First World War, and a branch was opened in Cambridge. It closed down in 1942.

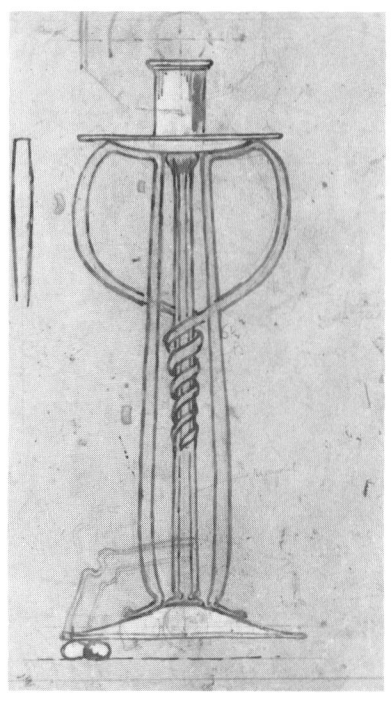

186 Nelson Dawson – Design for a candlestick, 1906.

EDWARD SPENCER (1872–1938)

British metalworker and designer

Spencer worked with Nelson Dawson and became a junior designer in his Artificers' Guild which was founded in 1901. He became chief designer for the Guild when it was acquired by Montague Fordham and transferred to Maddox Street. He developed a style very close to that of one of Fordham's most favoured and successful artists, J. Paul Cooper, and his later work is somewhat repetitive. The metalwork made for the Guild was widely publicised through illustrations in *The Studio* and through frequent exhibiting, and the venture was amongst the few commercially successful craft guilds, surviving until 1942.

ERNEST GIMSON (1864–1919)

British architect and designer

Born in Leicester, the son of Joseph Gimson, an engineer who founded the Leicester engineering works Gimson and Co. Gimson was articled at the age of seventeen to a local architect,

187 Ernest Gimson – Oak cupboard, panelled decoration, c. 1910.

Isaac Barradale. While he was with Barradale he studied part-time at the Leicester School of Art. When William Morris visited Leicester in 1884 to lecture at the Secularist Society (a visit arranged by Gimson's father who was a prominent member of the Society) Gimson met him, and on Morris's advice he went to London to enter the office of J. D. Sedding. While in Sedding's office Gimson occupied his spare time in acquiring a knowledge of traditional crafts, particularly that of decorative plasterwork, the only one — with the exception of turned wood, rush-seated chairs — with which he was to become thoroughly familiar, and one of the only crafts which he practised to any great extent. The cabinet making for which he is renowned was carried out under his direction and supervision by trained craftsmen, as was the iron and steel working, which was the work of a remarkable blacksmith called Alfred Bucknell. While in Sedding's office Gimson became friendly with his fellow-student Ernest Barnsley, and through him met his brother Sidney, then a pupil of Norman Shaw, as well as other members of the staff in Shaw's office including W. R. Lethaby, Reginald Blomfield and Mervyn Macartney. Together with these new friends he set up Kenton and Company, furniture designers and makers, in 1890. In 1891 he carried out a complex scheme of plaster decoration at Avon Tyrell, the house designed for Lord Manners by Lethaby, and in 1893 he did the plasterwork at the 'Hurst', another of Lethaby's houses.

After the collapse of Kenton and Co. in 1892 Gimson and the Barnsleys went to Gloucestershire where, in 1894, they set up a workshop in a fine Elizabethan house, Pinbury Park, near Cirencester. For some years after the establishment of the Pinbury workshop Gimson concentrated on his architectural work, designing the alterations to the house and executing the decorative plasterwork himself as well as a small number of private houses, including Daneway House, Sapperton, for his own occupation. Being, like the Barnsleys, of independent means Gimson was not under any pressure to earn his living, and he seems to have used these years as a fallow period, doing a certain amount of furniture designing which was to prove valuable when the larger workshops at Sapperton were opened later. In 1901 he engaged Peter van der Waals, a cabinet maker of Dutch extraction, as foreman-in-charge of his workshops, and in 1902 the move to the workshops at Daneway House, Sapperton was completed. Here, with the assistance of a group of skilled craftsmen under the direction of Peter Waals, Gimson's designs were executed. The workshops at Daneway House closed at the time of Gimson's death in 1919, but a number of the craftsmen went with Waals to his new establishment at Chalford and Gimson's designs were still used for some years after his death.

KENTON AND COMPANY

Furniture designers and makers

Kenton and Company was established in 1890 by Ernest Gimson, W. R. Lethaby, Sidney Barnsley, Reginald Blomfield and Mervyn Macartney. Four or five cabinet makers were employed and the work was carried out under the personal supervision of the artist. The inspiration for this venture came from Morris and Co., but the firm was undercapitalised and in spite of the success of the exhibition held at Barnard's Inn, the premises of the Art Workers' Guild, in 1891, Kenton and Company failed in the following year. Furniture made by the firm was used at Avon Tyrell and at Stanmore Hall, Lethaby's two major decorating commissions executed while the firm was in existence. Gimson's designs for the firm are a foretaste of his later work, indicating the characteristic geometry and style of surface decoration which combine to make his furniture so recognisable.

SIDNEY BARNSLEY (1865–1926)

British architect and furniture designer

Born in Birmingham, Sidney Barnsley was articled — about 1886 — to Richard Norman Shaw. He met Ernest Gimson through his brother, a fellow pupil in the office of J. D. Sedding, and in 1890 joined them in founding Kenton and Co. At this date he was sharing rooms with Gimson in London. After the failure of Kenton and Co. he moved with Gimson to Gloucestershire where he set up his own small workshop, making up his furniture designs. After Gimson's death he made little more furniture as he was fully occupied with realising Gimson's unfinished architectural work, including his projected memorial library at Bedales School.

ERNEST BARNSLEY (1863–1926)

British architect and designer

Originally articled by J. D. Sedding, Ernest Barnsley established an architectural practice in Birmingham in 1892, but went to Gloucestershire to join his brother and Ernest Gimson in 1893 where he continued his architectural career and designed and made furniture mostly for his own houses. For two years he was in partnership with Gimson at the Daneway workshops, but gave it up to concentrate on his architectural work, much of which was for the influential Society for the Protection of Ancient Buildings.

Ernest and Sidney Barnsley were two of the younger sons of one of the partners in John Barnsley and Sons, who built the Birmingham Town Hall which was designed by Hansom

188 Ernest Gimson – Cabinet on a stand, the door panels inset with pierced gesso ornaments, *c.* 1910.

188

189

190

189 Gustav Stickley – Interior with Craftsman Workshops furniture, c. 1910.

190 Roycroft Copper Shop – Hand-hammered copper inkwell with glass liner, c. 1915.

191 Gustav Stickley – Oak side chair with inlays of darker wood, copper and pewter, designed by Harvey Ellis and made by United Crafts, Syracuse, N.Y., 1903.

146

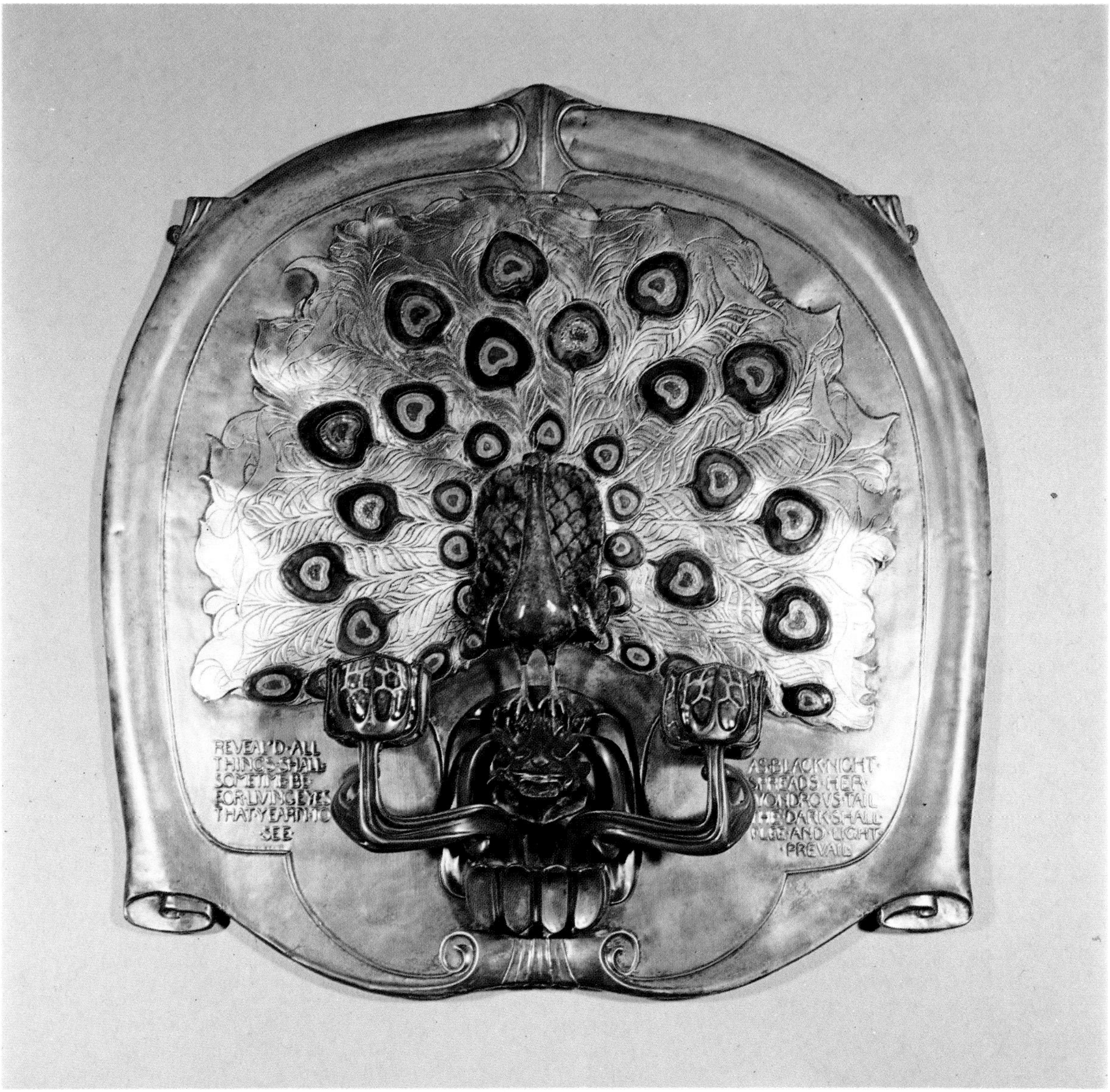

192

193

192 Alexander Fisher – Lighting sconce, with two branching candle holders, peacock enamelled in naturalistic colours. Shown at the Arts and Crafts Exhibition in 1896.

193 Henry Wilson – Detail of hair ornament in silver and gold with inset plique-à-jour enamels set with mother-of-pearl and semi-precious stones, c. 1902.

(patentee of the two-wheeled cabriolet, 1834). All three were members of the Society for the Protection of Ancient Buildings, Morris's 'Anti-Scrape', a society which had a far greater effect on the architecture of the nineteenth century than is generally recognised.

PETER VAN DER WAALS (1870–1937)

Dutch furniture designer and craftsman

Peter van der Waals was born in The Hague in Holland and worked as a cabinet maker in Holland, Belgium, Germany and Austria before coming to London in 1899. In 1900 he answered an advertisement for the post of chief cabinet maker in the workshops which Gimson was just setting up in Cirencester — a post which he received. He remained with Gimson until the latter's death in 1919, having become a vital influence in determining the style of the furniture produced in the Daneway Workshops at Sapperton. In 1920 he set up his own workshops at Chalford intending to start a new venture, but he employed a number of the craftsmen from Daneway and even continued to produce some of Gimson's old designs as well as designs of his own. Therefore it would be idle to pretend that his own furniture represents any real advance from the characteristic style employed by Gimson. He died at Chalford in 1937 and the following year a disastrous fire in his workshops destroyed all his designs and probably a number of Gimson's designs as well.

GUSTAV STICKLEY (1857–1942)

American designer and metalworker

Gustav Stickley was born in Wisconsin and trained as a stonemason. He moved to Pennsylvania in 1876 and was apprenticed to his uncle, who made plain chairs with cane seats, and then to other relatives. In 1898 he visited Europe, meeting Voysey and other designers in England, and on his return formed the Gustav Stickley Company in Eastwood, near Syracuse, New York. In 1900 he exhibited at Grand Rapids and the same year enlarged the company, which became the Craftsman Workshops, with their own timber mills in the Adirondacks. He exhibited at the Pan-American Exposition in Buffalo in 1905, sharing a stand with the Grueby Faience Co. From October 1901 to December 1916 he published *The Craftsman*. From April 1903 to January 1904 the designer-architect Harvey Ellis worked for him, ornamenting furniture with inlaid metals. From 1902 they also produced metalwork. In 1905 the administrative office was moved to New York, but the firm went bankrupt and was taken over by L. and J. G. Stickley in April 1915 as the Stickley Manufacturing Co. which still exists today.

STICKLEY BROTHERS

American furniture makers and designers
Charles Stickley went into furniture business with his uncle in
New York state in 1889. George and Albert Stickley
established Stickley Bros. Co. in Grand Rapids in 1891.
Leopold and J. George Stickley left the Craftsman Workshops
in 1900 to form their own company in Fayetteville, New York.
They executed furniture for Frank Lloyd Wright in 1900.

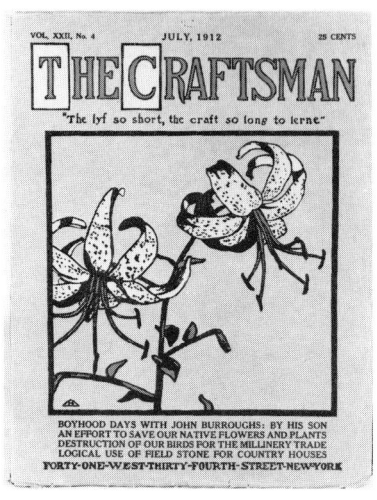

194 Cover of *The Craftsman*, Vol.
XXII, No. 4 July 1912.

ELBERT HUBBARD AND THE ROYCROFTERS

American printer and founder of arts and crafts community
Elbert Hubbard (1856–1915) sold his partnership in a soap
company in 1893 and settled in East Aurora, near Buffalo,
New York. In 1892 he had visited the Kelmscott Press in
England and met Morris. The following year, having bought a
small press, he published his magazine the *Philistine* to be
followed by *The Song of Songs*. A bindery was followed by a
leather shop and then, in 1901, a furniture shop. Hubbard was
not a designer but Roycroft became an artistic community
with lectures by Hubbard, an apprenticeship system and
various facilities.

In 1903 Dard Hunter came to East Aurora and subsequently
set up his own studio for designing furniture, metalwork and
leaded glass. In 1908 he went to Vienna and again in 1910,
when he returned to set up his independent School of
Handicraft. The head of the Copper Shop was an Austrian,
Karl Kipp, who had been a banker but joined the Roycrofters
from 1908 to 1912, when he also left to form his own
workshop, the Tookay Shop. In 1915 the Hubbards
disappeared on the Lusitania and the shops continued under
Bert Hubbard until their sale in 1938.

ROSE VALLEY ASSOCIATION

American craft community
The community was started in 1901 by the Philadelphia
architect William L. Price (1861–1916) and M. Hawley
McLanahan in old mill buildings in Moylan, fourteen miles
from the centre of Philadelphia. Based on the ideals of Morris's
News from Nowhere and on Ashbee's Guild of Handicraft at
Chipping Campden, they produced pottery and furniture,
with a sales outlet in Philadelphia. There was also a Village
Press and from 1903 to 1907 they published the *Artsman*
magazine. The community went bankrupt in 1909.

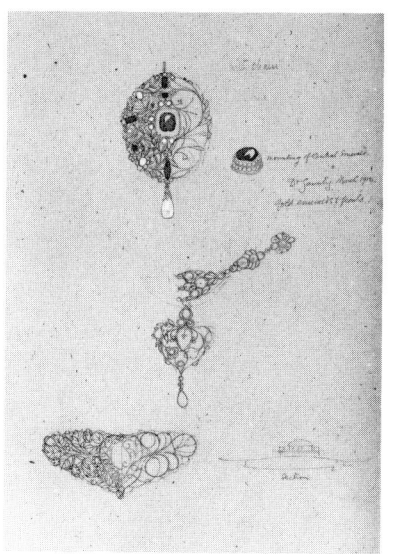

BIRMINGHAM GUILD OF HANDICRAFT

The Birmingham Guild was established in 1890 by local admirers of Ruskin and Morris, with Montague Fordham as one of the first directors. W. H. Bidlake, the architect, was an honorary director. The Guild employed about twenty craftsmen and occupied a mediaeval building, Kyrle Hall, in Sheep Street in Birmingham. Pressure of work forced the Guild to expand and in 1895 it became a limited company. Arthur Dixon (1856–1929), the metalworker, was the chief designer for the Guild and he wrote a summary of the Guild's aims and ideals for *The Quest* (Vol. II), a quarterly magazine hand-printed on the premises in Sheep Street. In 1910 financial problems were resolved by amalgamation with the metalworking firm of E. & R. Gittins, who made fine jewellery as well as the architectural metalwork in which the Guild specialised. The Guild is still in existence, and has added agricultural and light engineering work to the architectural work which they still do.

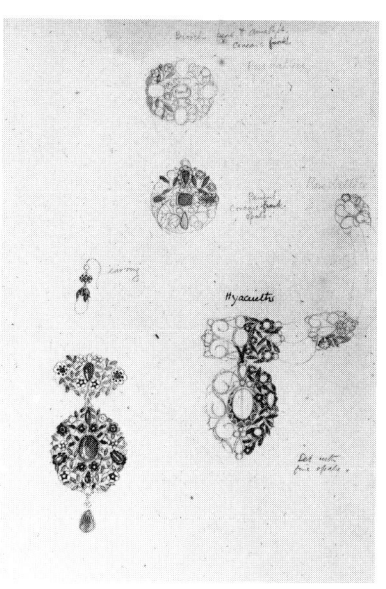

195, 196 Arthur Gaskin – Designs for jewellery, 1908-12.

ARTHUR JOSEPH GASKIN (1862–1928)

Painter, graphic artist, jewellery designer and enamellist
Gaskin studied at the Birmingham School of Art under E. R. Taylor and subsequently taught there. In 1894 he married fellow student Georgina Cave France with whom he started a joint venture in 1899 designing and making jewellery and silverwork.

Gaskin participated with fellow Birmingham artists C. M. Gere and Bernard Sleigh in the revival of wood-engraving. He illustrated a number of books including Hans Christian Andersen's *Stories and Fairytales* (1893) and *Household Tales* (1899) by the Brothers Grimm. In 1896 he illustrated Edmund Spenser's *Shepheardes Callender* for the Kelmscott Press. The designs were so successful that Morris omitted the borders which he usually designed for the Kelmscott book illustrations, and the powerful linear woodcuts fill the page without the need for further embellishment.

Extensive experiments with the use of tempera as a medium for painting, before the work involved in the metalworking venture, forced him virtually to abandon his career as a painter. He became head of the recently founded Vittoria Street School for jewellers and silversmiths in Birmingham in 1902. Gaskin retired from Birmingham in 1925 and went to work in the Cotswolds. He died in Chipping Campden in Gloucestershire.

BROMSGROVE GUILD OF APPLIED ART

The Bromsgrove Guild was founded c. 1890 by Walter Gilbert, cousin of the sculptor Alfred Gilbert, by whom he was greatly influenced. It specialised in metalwork and jewellery. Gaskin (q.v.) and Prof. Joseph Hodel both designed work for the Guild. The Guild exhibited at the Paris Centennial Exhibition in 1900.

YATTENDON METALWORKING CLASS

The class was started in 1890 as a brass-working course by Mrs Alfred Waterhouse, (wife of the great Victorian architect), of Yattendon Court, Berkshire, to give occupation to the men of the village in the evening. It was soon discovered that copper was easier and more pleasant to work and therefore only the very early work is in brass. The men worked once a week in the evening from 7 p.m. until 9.30 or 10, the older teaching the younger. The designs were almost all made by Mrs Waterhouse using garden plants and foliage for inspiration. All the materials were provided by her and the workmen received payment for each piece as it was sold.

The class-work was exhibited at the Home Arts and Industries Exhibition at the Royal Albert Hall and sold through a shop in the village run by Mrs Wyatt in a house called 'Pargeters'. As the work of the class became known some special commissions were executed — among them some ecclesiastical works such as font covers. Some of the copper-work was sold at Liberty's. The class was disbanded in 1914 at the outbreak of the First World War.

GRUEBY FAIENCE COMPANY

American art pottery company

The Grueby Faience Company was founded in Boston by William H. Grueby (born 1867) in 1894, after he had trained at the J. and J. G. Low Art Tile Works in Chelsea, after the failure of an earlier company of his own. The company made architectural faience and pottery. After seeing the work of Delaherche at the Chicago World's Fair of 1893, Grueby started to use a matt glaze in 1898 which was usually dark green. In 1899 Grueby Pottery was separated from the rest of the original company and in 1908 the firm went bankrupt, though it reformed under the name of Grueby Faience and Tile Co. No vases were exhibited after this time and production appears to have ceased about 1911. Grueby died in 1925, but the firm had been sold in 1919 to a tile manufactory. Grueby

197 George Grant Elmslie - Bronze plated cast iron ornamental medallion, 1899, for the elevator doors of the Carson, Pirie, Scott and Co. Department Store designed by Louis Sullivan.

was responsible for popularising matt glazes in America and his designs were admired for their restraint, especially in comparison with the influences of Art Nouveau, using often the simplest leaf motifs.

GEORGE GRANT ELMSLIE (1871–1952)

American architect and interior designer

Born in Scotland, Elmslie emigrated to the United States in 1884. He entered the offices of the architect J. S. Silsbee in 1887, and there met Frank Lloyd Wright and G. W. Maher. In 1889 he moved to the offices of Adler and Sullivan and became chief designer in 1895. He set up his own practice in 1909 in partnership with W. G. Purcell and G. Frick, who died in 1913, although Elmslie and Purcell continued until 1922. Elmslie only designed furniture for his most important interiors, using mainly oak. He also designed leaded glass, textiles and terracotta ornaments.

NEWCOMB COLLEGE POTTERY

American art pottery school

The pottery was started on an experimental basis in 1895 in what had been the women's division of Tulane University, New Orleans. The first students came from the Baronne Street Pottery led by William Woodward. Woodward's brother Ellsworth became the Director of Newcomb with Mary G. Shearer, who had been associated with the women who founded Rookwood, as instructor of design and Joseph Meyer as technician and potter. The idea was to train women in some useful craft and the artists were encouraged to sign their work. Low-fired bisque ware was produced, often with incised carving, with the conventionalised designs influenced by the southern landscape and flora. In 1910 Paul E. Cox developed a matt glaze for the pottery, following the direction popular at the time. The College housed both students and graduates employed on a professional basis. Until 1918 the pottery was thrown by professional potters, but then an experimental laboratory was opened and the women artists could then control the entire process. The pottery ceased production in 1931.

198 George Grant Elmslie – Side chair in oak, made for the Charles A. Purcell house, Illinois, 1909.

199

199 J.D. Sedding – Interior of Holy Trinity Church, Sloane Street.

200 Henry Wilson – Chancel gates at Holy Trinity Church, Sloane Street, *c*. 1892.

201 Henry Wilson – Gold pendant and chain in Renaissance style, with green enamel columns, moonstones and a beryl, the whole dependant from a chalcedony bead with pearl clusters. Designed and made for David Strachan, the stained glass artist, *c*. 1910.

202 Henry Wilson – Design for a hair ornament with enamel insets, *c*. 1905.

203 Nelson Dawson and Edith Dawson – Steel and copper presentation casket with inset enamels and cabochon turquoises, inscribed 'BARUM' and dated 1896.

200

201

202

203

204

204 Edward Spencer – Silver claret jug set with stones, c. 1905.

Opposite
205 Grueby Pottery – Pottery vase with dark green and yellow matt glazes, c. 1902.

Page 158
206 *(left)* Artus Van Briggle – Vase in iridescent colours; *(left centre)* Grueby Faience Company – Vase with matt green glaze, c. 1900; *(right centre)* Rookwood Pottery – 'Wisteria' vase, c. 1901; *(right)* Rookwood Pottery – 'Fressia' vase, c. 1901.

207 Della Robbia Pottery Co. – Two-handled vase with sgraffito decoration, c. 1900.

208 Grueby Faience Co. – Vase with a matt green glaze. This model was shown at the Centennial Exhibition in 1900.

Page 159
209 J. Paul Cooper – 'The Legend of Perseus and Andromeda'. Pair of silver candlesticks decorated with chased and repoussé work, 1913.

210 Omar Ramsden and Alwyn Carr – Silver tea caddy with repoussé galleon on the lid, 1913.

211 Omar Ramsden and Alwyn Carr – Pair of silver candlesticks, 1907.

206

207

208

209

210

211

212

213

212 Ernest Gimson – Cabinet of drawers, inlaid with cherry and bone, *c.* 1910.

213 Ernest Gimson – Ebony box with lid, inlaid with silver and ivory, *c.* 1910.

214 Sidney Barnsley – Oak dresser, *c.* 1910.

215 Ernest Gimson – Walnut sideboard with ebony backrail, feet and stretchers, inlaid with holly and ebony stringing, the handles by Alfred Bucknell, *c.* 1910.

214

215

216

217

216 Gustav Stickley – Group of furniture from the Craftsman Workshops, *c.* 1910.

217 Gustav Stickley – Oak rocking chair with a leather seat, Craftsman Workshops, 1904-6.

218 Gustav Stickley – Oak music cabinet, *c.* 1910-12.

219 Roycroft Shops – Oak magazine pedestal, showing Roycroft mark, *c.* 1912.

220 Gustav Stickley – Oak trestle table, Craftsman Workshops, *c.* 1912. This was not the standard size trestle table and was perhaps made to order.

218

219

220

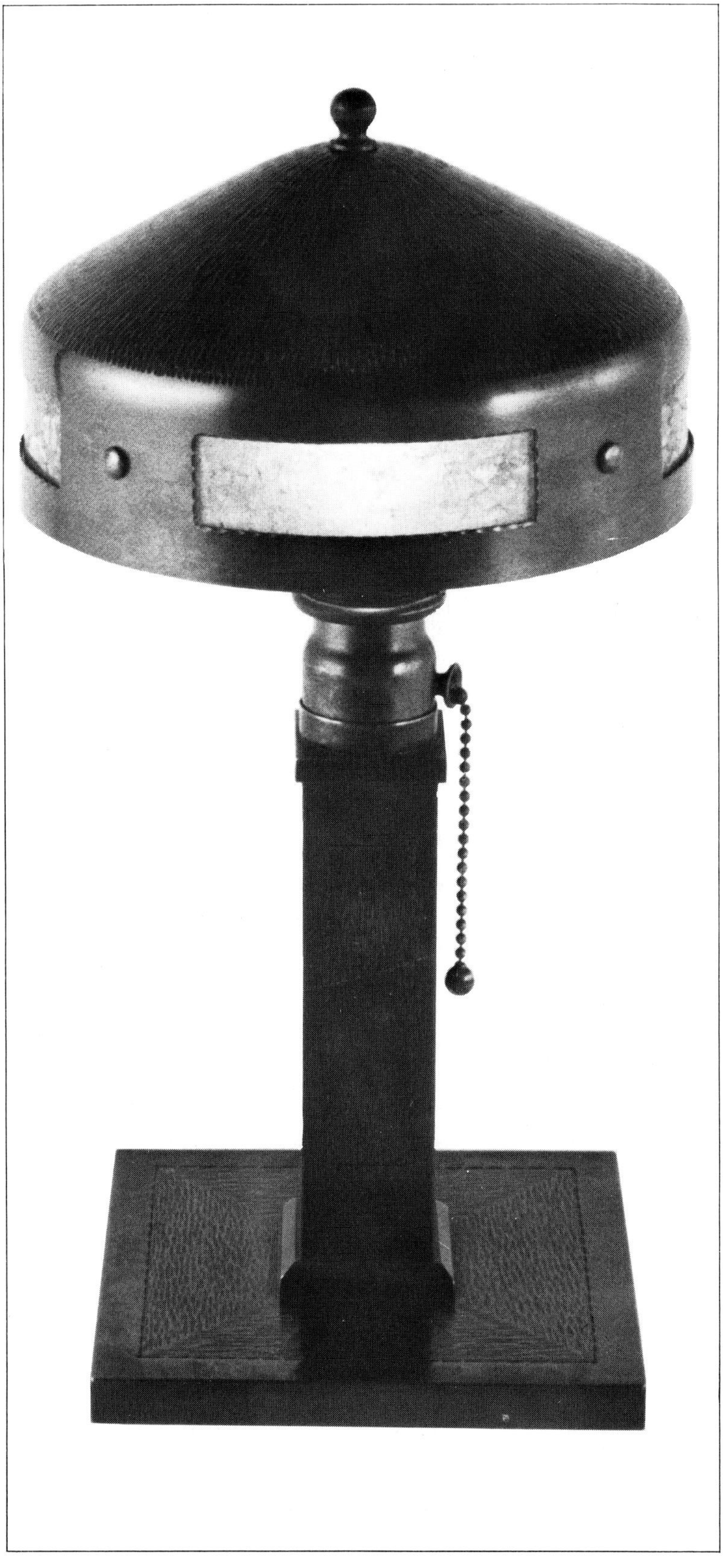

222

221 Roycroft Shops – Desk lamp in hand-hammered copper with mica shades, *c.* 1904-12. The same lamp appeared in a 1910 photograph of Elbert Hubbard sitting at his desk.

222 The Buffalo Pottery – Semi-vitreous pottery dinner plate with hand-painted underglaze decoration, made for the Roycroft Shops, *c.* 1910-12.

223 Arthur Dixon – Kettle and stand designed for the Birmingham Guild of Handicraft, 1905.

221

223

224

225

226

227

224 Grueby Faience Co. – Pottery vase by Ruth Ericson. 10⅝in. high, *c.* 1900.

225 Grueby Faience Co. – Glazed pottery vase, 7½in. high, *c.* 1898.

226 Newcomb College Pottery – Glazed pottery and painted vase made by Joseph Meyer, 5⁷/₁₆in. high, *c.* 1904.

227 Newcomb College Pottery – Glazed and painted pottery vase made by Joseph Meyer, 5½in. high, *c.* 1904.

228

228 Grueby Faience Co. – Landscape tile, *c.* 1906.

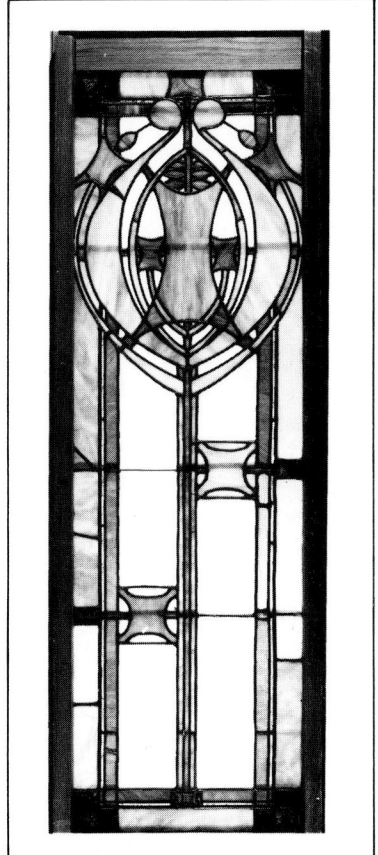

229 George Grant Elmslie – Leaded stained glass window, 63 × 15 in., 1911.

230 George Grant Elmslie (attrib.) – Tall mahogany clock with brass inlay, 1912.

229   230

5 ARTS AND CRAFTS AND THE BEGINNINGS OF MODERNISM

Neither the 'Glasgow Four' nor Frank Lloyd Wright can be regarded as in any way members of the Arts and Crafts Movement, yet it was through their pioneer design work that the craft ethic could be retranslated into the ideology of the Modern Movement. It can thus be seen, for example, that Voysey's significance for the Modern Movement came largely through his influence on Mackintosh. The Glasgow school artists made more extensive and more valuable contacts abroad than the craft revivalists, and there is a visible cross-fertilization of ideas between the Secessionists in Vienna and the Glasgow decorative school. Thus were the ideals of Morris and Ashbee, which were eagerly listened to on the Continent, made aesthetically acceptable within the more stylised framework of decorative design in Austria and Germany. The English rejection of the work of the Glasgow school heralded the beginnings of British provincialism in matters of design whose effects are still felt today. For the Americans, Frank Lloyd Wright performed the same aesthetic function as the 'Glasgow Four'; through him the ideas of Gustav Stickley — and thus, by extension, of Morris — were transmuted into a twentieth-century idiom, but with the significant difference that in America his work was eagerly accepted and assimilated.

Robert Judson Clark said of Frank Lloyd Wright '[His] ideas about architecture and the decorative arts were derived from the Arts and Crafts Movement, to which his early work was in turn a substantial contribution' (in *The Arts and Crafts Movement in America* p. 68), thus echoing Fra Newbery's reported remarks on C. R. Mackintosh's debt to C. F. A. Voysey. It is instructive to compare the work of these two men and to see that within the framework of the Arts and Crafts idiom they both arrived at very similar solutions. C. R. Mackintosh came to exaggerate his forms in a way that drove him towards continental Art Nouveau whereas F. L. Wright was not diverted away from the logical progression towards the Modern Style. In retrospect it can be seen that the stylistic excesses of Art Nouveau were bound to prove a cultural dead-end while the stripping-down process which marked the prelude to the Modern Movement left those artists who had betrayed the commitment to significant form with nothing of value to say.

231 C.R. Mackintosh – Light fitting with leaded coloured glass insets, c. 1902.

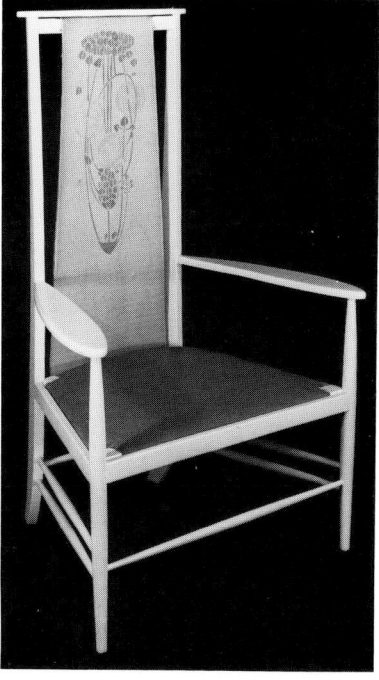

232 C.R. Mackintosh – Armchair, painted white and upholstered in linen, 1900.

CHARLES RENNIE MACKINTOSH (1868–1928)

Scottish architect and designer

Born in Glasgow, Mackintosh attended the Glasgow School of Art from 1885, remaining there as a part-time student after being apprenticed to a Glasgow architect, John Hutchison. In 1889 he joined the firm of Honeyman and Keppie and later became a partner, remaining with them until 1913. In 1896 the 'Glasgow Four' were invited to send work to the Arts and Crafts Exhibition Society where their posters were met with astonishment and distaste; a reaction which was to become familiar in England. The editor of *The Studio*, however, was sufficiently intrigued to visit Glasgow himself and wrote two articles on their work in 1897. Also in 1896 Mackintosh won the competition for the design of the new buildings for the Glasgow School of Art. From 1897 to 1916 he was occupied with designing, decorating and furnishing a chain of tea-rooms, established in Glasgow by the Misses Cranston as part of a campaign, started in the 1880s with the founding of the Glasgow Temperance Movement, to combat widespread daytime drunkenness. The tea-rooms were provided with billiard tables and smoking-rooms for the amusement of the customers but few, if any, of the Glasgow drunks patronised the new establishments with their elegant and original furniture and fittings.

During this same period the best of the private houses were designed, among them Hill House at Helensburgh for the publisher William Blackie, and Windyhill at Kilmacolm. In 1895 he exhibited at L'OEuvre Artistique in Liège. He exhibited with the Vienna Secession artists at their Eighth exhibition in 1900, and was commissioned by Wärndorfer, the banker — and later director — of the Wiener Werkstätte, to design a music salon for his house. He submitted a design, in 1901, to the competition devised by Zeitschrift fur Innendekoration for a *Haus der Kunstfreundes*, but it was disqualified on a technicality, and the winner was M. H. Baillie Scott. In 1902 he designed the Scottish Pavilion for the Exposizione Internazionale in Turin. Influence from his contacts in Vienna become evident in the West front of the School of Art which was built in 1907–9. He left Glasgow in 1913 and established himself in London, but little was achieved during this period, hardly more than a studio in Chelsea and the interior of 78 Derngate, the house belonging to J. Basset-Lowke in Northampton (*c*.1917). In 1920 he gave up architecture and moved to Port de Vendres in France where he devoted himself to painting. He died in London in 1928.

FRANK LLOYD WRIGHT (1867–1959)

American architect and designer

Frank Lloyd Wright was born in Wisconsin and studied civil

engineering at the University of Wisconsin as a special student. In 1887 he left for Chicago and worked for five months in the offices of Joseph L. Silsbee, where George W. Maher and George Grant Elmslie also worked. From 1888 to 1893 he worked in the offices of Adler and Sullivan, where he became chief draughtsman. When Wright left to form his own practice he shared offices in the Schiller Building (which he had helped Sullivan design) with Cecil Corwin, whom he had met in Silsbee's offices. When Corwin departed for the East, Wright moved to offices in Steinway Hall, which he shared with D. H. Perkins, R. C. Spencer and Myron Hunt, all of whom had studied at MIT. His first independent commission was the Winslow residence (1893) and his other early designs, such as the Willitts house, Highland Park, the Coonley house, Riverside, and the Robie house, Chicago, earned the title of 'prairie style'. The two earliest groups of furniture he designed were for his own house (1895) and for Isidore Holler (1897).

Wright's style was geometric and starkly functional with no applied ornament apart from the intrinsic juxtaposition of shape and form except in patterned leaded glass windows. He employed new constructional techniques, especially in his use of steel and reinforced concrete. Despite some early photographs of his own home, which show a rather typical Victorian-Aesthetic clutter, he advocated open-plan interiors and often designed the furniture and fittings to complement his schemes. In 1902 the annual exhibition of the Chicago Architectural Club was dominated by the work of Sullivan and Wright and his associates from Steinway Hall, although the change in style from conservative Queen Anne revival taste was not altogether warmly received.

From 1903 to 1908 Wright worked mainly at his Oak Park Studio, where many young architects came to work and study with him. The renderings completed during this period were published by Ernst Wasmuth in Berlin in 1910, with a foreword by C. R. Ashbee: *Ausgefuehrte Bauten und Entwuerfe von Frank Lloyd Wright*. Although the book was enthusiastically seized upon in Europe it was criticised in America for the starkness of design. Many of Wright's designs were published in the *Ladies Home Journal* in America and show his developing maturity after 1900. In 1905 he visited Japan and in 1909 left for Europe with his mistress. On his return he settled in Wisconsin, spending time also in California and Japan. Many of his former clients turned to his pupils from Oak Park for their commissions and Wright felt some bitterness towards the Chicago School. He continued to work all over the U.S.A. until his death and was a vital influence on European architecture.

233 Frank Lloyd Wright – Stained glass window from the Dana residence, Springfield, Illinois, 1902.

J. HERBERT MACNAIR (1868–1955)

Scottish architect and designer
Born in Glasgow, MacNair was educated at the Collegiate

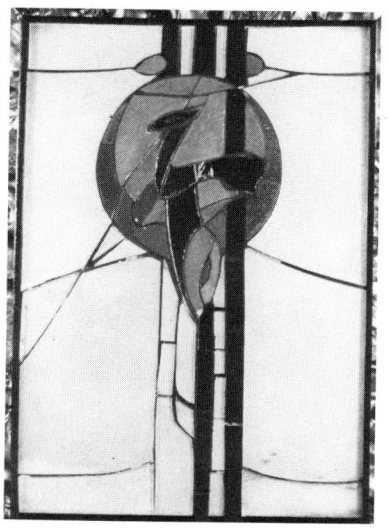

234 Jessie M. King – Leaded, mirrored and coloured glass mosaic panel, 'The Enchanted Faun', c. 1908.

School, Greenock, and went to Rouen to study painting only after overcoming opposition from his father who wished him to become an engineer. In 1888 he started an apprenticeship with the Glasgow architect John Honeyman, who early in the following year formed a partnership with John Keppie. Shortly afterwards C. R. Mackintosh (q.v.) joined the firm as a draughtsman. MacNair was not particularly happy in the study of architecture and during quiet periods in the office he occupied himself making designs for furniture. As part of the training for architecture MacNair had to attend evening classes at the Glasgow School of Art and it was in about 1893, through the headmaster, Fra Newbery, that he and Mackintosh met the Macdonald sisters who had been attending a daytime course at the School since 1891. In 1895, shortly after completing the course at the School of Art, MacNair left Honeyman and Keppie and opened his own business at 227 West George Street in Glasgow, specialising in the design of furniture, book-illustration, book-plates and posters. In 1897 he was offered a post at Liverpool University as Instructor in Design at the School of Architecture and Applied Art. He returned briefly to Glasgow to marry Frances Macdonald in 1899.

In Liverpool he undertook a number of decorating commissions in addition to his teaching, and in 1902 he designed the Writing Room for the Scottish Pavilion at the Exposizione Internazionale in Turin with his wife. The interiors of his own house, 54 Oxford Street, Liverpool, were illustrated in *The Studio* volume on 'Modern British Domestic Architecture' in 1901, and can be seen to be his most ambitious and important work. In 1905 the University Art School closed down and after teaching for three years at the Sandon Studios Society which was founded to replace it, MacNair returned with his wife to Glasgow. Here their only income was provided by Frances MacNair's teaching job at the School of Art, supplemented on occasion by the money from casual jobs undertaken by MacNair. After his wife's death in 1921 MacNair retired into total obscurity, finally dying in an old people's home where he had gone after the death of his sister. He destroyed a large amount of both his own and his wife's work and such pieces as have survived mostly belonged to family and friends.

GEORGE WALTON (1867–1933)

Scottish architect and interior designer

Walton attended evening classes at the Glasgow School of Art before setting up in business as a designer and decorator (George Walton and Co. Ecclesiastical and House Decorators) in Glasgow in 1888. He exhibited with the Art and Crafts Society in 1890. Having decorated a number of houses in the Glasgow area, he moved to London in 1897. From 1897 to 1902 he was occupied with the designing of furniture and fitments and shop-fronts for branches of the Kodak camera company in Brussels, Glasgow, Milan, Moscow, Vienna, Leningrad and London. In 1898 he opened a subsidiary branch of his business in York. He was architect and designer to The Central Liquor Traffic Board from 1916 to 1921, and later designed fabrics for Morton Sundour in the late 1920s.

ERNEST ARCHIBALD TAYLOR (1874–1951)

Scottish furniture and stained glass designer

E. A. Taylor was born in Greenock, the fifteenth of the seventeen children of a major in the Royal Artillery. He was trained as a draughtsman in the yards of the shipbuilders and engineers, Scott and Co. Ltd., before going to the Glasgow School of Art in the 1890s. Inevitably he came under the influence of the powerful 'Four' — Mackintosh, J. H. MacNair and Frances and Margaret Macdonald. In about 1900 he joined the well-established Glasgow cabinet making firm, Wylie and Lockhead Ltd., and designed a drawing-room for their pavilion at the 1901 Glasgow International Exhibition. In 1902 he joined his fellow Glasgow School artists in exhibiting at Turin where he won a diploma and a medal. Until his marriage and removal to Manchester in 1908, Taylor also taught at the School of Art and at a Glasgow Technical College. In Manchester he worked as a designer for George Wragge Ltd., a firm of decorators with other branches in Glasgow and London.

Before leaving Glasgow E. A. Taylor had executed two important private commissions which came to him as a result of his work for Wylie and Lockhead shown at the Glasgow Exhibition. The work on 32 Radnor Road, Birmingham for Mrs Margaret Coats, whose husband was a member of the Paisley thread-manufacturing family, was undertaken in 1901, and three of the room settings from this scheme have recently been acquired by the Glasgow Museum and Art Gallery. The work on the Pollockshields house of William Douglas Weir (later Lord Weir) was done in 1901/2. From this time until 1914 Taylor was much occupied with stained glass design and from 1911–14 with teaching and organizing at the Shealing Atelier of Fine Art which he and his wife, Jessie King (q.v.) established in Paris at 16 rue de la Grande-Chaumière. In 1914 the outbreak of war forced him to return to Scotland and he spent the rest of his life there. In 1920 he more or less gave up designing and devoted his time to teaching, writing and painting.

JESSIE M. KING (1873–1949)

Scottish designer and illustrator

The daughter of a minister, Jessie King was brought up in

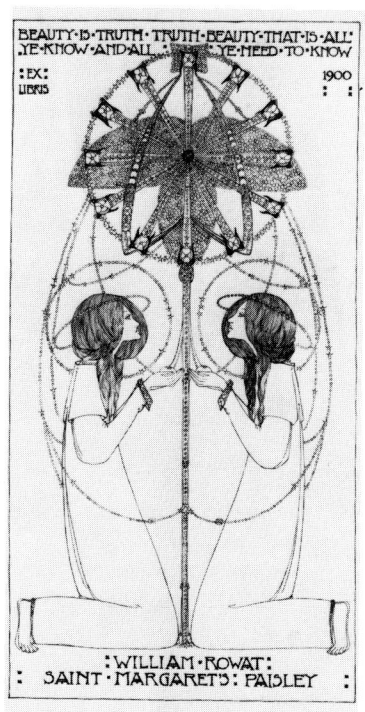

235 Jessie M. King – Design for a bookplate for William Rowat, with a quotation from Keats, 1900.

Branden, near Glasgow, and was only allowed to attend the Glasgow School of Art after overcoming the opposition of both her parents. While still a student and showing great promise as a graphic artist, she produced 'a short history of the school' illuminated on vellum, which was ceremoniously buried with the laying of the foundation stone for the new School of Art in 1898, designed by C. R. Mackintosh. She became a lecturer in book decoration at the School of Art and in 1902 participated in the design and decoration of Mackintosh's Scottish Pavilion at the Exposizione Nazionale in Turin, and there won a gold medal for a book cover, a re-binding of *L'Evangile de l'Enfance* carried out in gold-tooled white vellum by Maclehose of Glasgow. Though best known for her work in book design and illustration she also worked for Liberty's, designing for the 'Cymric' range of silver and for the fabric department. She experimented with batik work and later with hand-painted pottery.

In 1908 she married E. A. Taylor, the furniture designer and one-time fellow student at the School of Art. They went to live in Salford so that Taylor could continue with his designing job in Manchester. By 1911 they were established in Paris with a studio in the rue de la Grande-Chaumière. At the outbreak of war in 1914 they returned to Kirkcudbright, Scotland and here Jessie King pursued her interest in batik work which had been aroused during the years in Paris. She designed and made dresses and scarves, and ran classes in her studio in the technique of decorating with dye in the traditional batik manner. Jessie King continued to work and to exhibit right up to the time of her death, evolving a more schematic style during the twenties and thirties which owed less to the Mackintosh/Macdonald influence, so apparent in her earlier work. She died in Scotland on 3 August 1949.

GEORGE LOGAN (fl. *c.* 1900–1914)

Scottish furniture designer

Working from 1900, Logan was employed by the well-established firm of Glasgow cabinet-makers, Wylie and Lockhead, and with E. A. Taylor and John Ednie he participated in the designing of the Wylie and Lockhead pavilion for the Glasgow International Exhibition in 1901 (Logan was responsible for the bedroom). In 1902 he again exhibited with E. A. Taylor, in the third appartment on the Glasgow stand at the International Exhibition of Modern Decorative Art at Turin. This section included work by Jessie King as well as that of Taylor and Logan, and Logan's screen had a decorative panel by Jessie King inserted into the central leaf. The first 'appartment' contained Mackintosh's 'Rose Bower', the second, MacNair's 'Lady's Writing Room'. Thus it is not necessary to look any further to find the source of

Logan's inspiration, but — like E. A. Taylor and George Walton — he commonly used a conventional framework and set of proportions for his furniture designs, more suited to the commercial nature of his work for Wylie and Lockhead than the eccentric, elongated shapes, and unconventional use of structural elements which is found in the work of the 'Four'.

JESSIE R. NEWBERY (born 1864)

Scottish designer, embroideress and teacher
Jessie Newbery was the daughter of William Rowat, a manufacturer of Paisley shawls. In 1889 she married Francis H. Newbery, the principal of the Glasgow School of Art. Around the date of her marriage Mackintosh decorated a house in Glasgow owned by her family. From 1894 to 1908 she taught embroidery at the School of Art and influenced many of the students to consider it as a serious form, among them the Macdonald sisters and Ann Macbeth. She continued to do a great deal of embroidery after she had given up teaching, as well as some textile design.

236 Jessie R. Newbery – Cushion cover in embroidered linen, 1899.

ANNE MACBETH (1875–1948)

Designer, embroideress and teacher
Anne Macbeth was a member of the 'Glasgow School' and a teacher at the Glasgow School of Art for many years. She executed a number of ecclesiastical commissions for embroidery, and published an instructional manual called *Educational Needlecraft* which was widely influential. She also established an embroidery class for children at the School of Art, which sought to inculcate a feeling for colour and design from an early age. She devised a system of working with bold designs in many colours which was a happy contrast to the intensely boring and eye-straining discipline of white work — the mainstay of most sewing instruction throughout the nineteenth century. Embroidered panels executed by herself and her pupils decorated many Glasgow interiors, though little has survived. However, illustrations in contemporary periodicals, notably *The Studio*, give a good idea of her great talent for embroidery design.

237 Anne Macbeth – Detail from a tablecloth in embroidered linen, c. 1900.

Opposite
238 C.R. Mackintosh – Chair, painted white, and upholstered in linen, 1900.

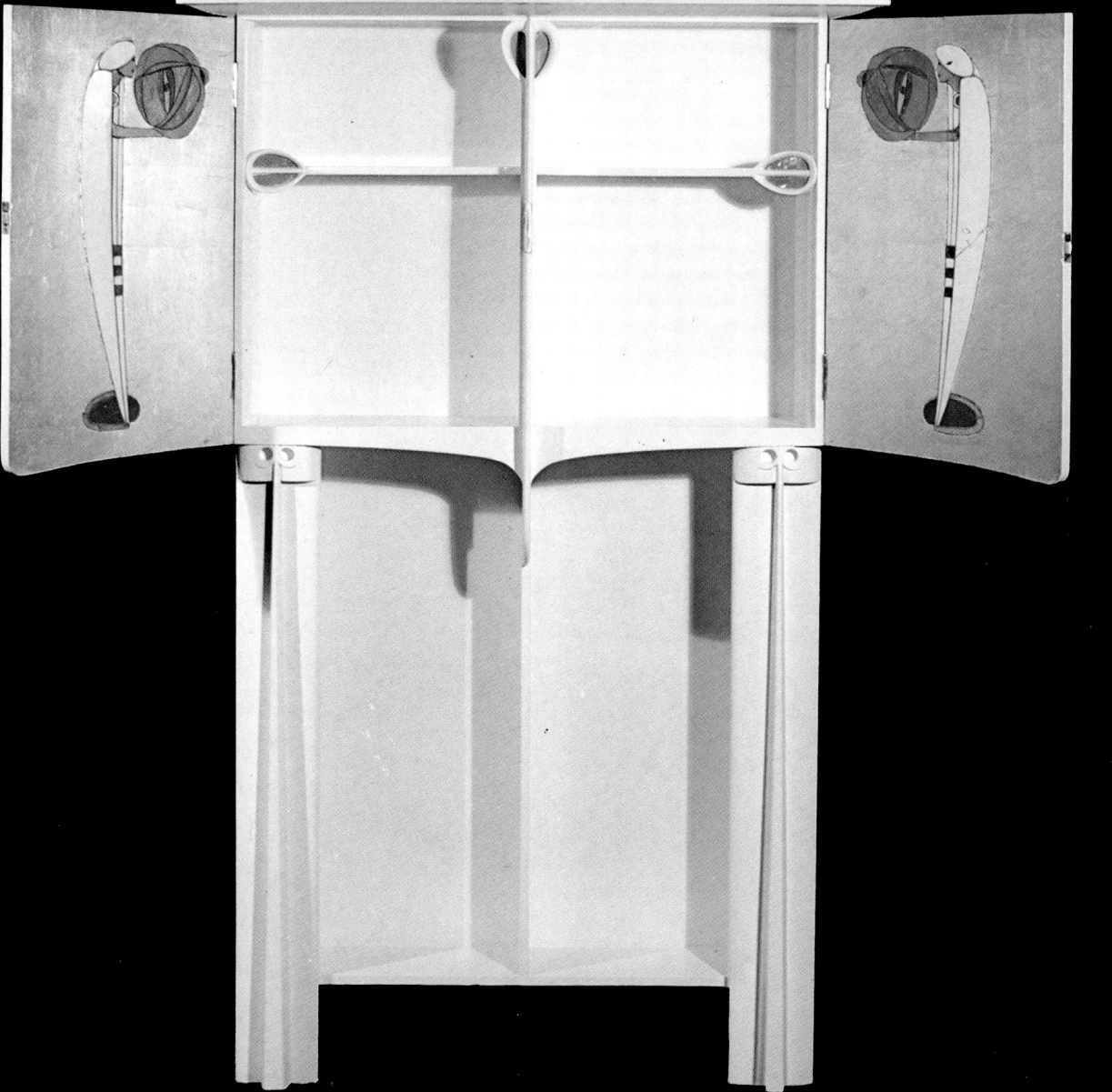

239 C.R. Mackintosh – Cabinet
in white painted wood with
metal handles, the inside door panels
painted silver, 1902.

240 C.R. Mackintosh – Linen press in
cypress wood with a light stain finish
and brass fittings, c. 1893.

240

241

241 C.R. Mackintosh – Oak hall table with a green stain finish, *c.* 1900.

242 C.R. Mackintosh – Oak table with a dark stain finish, *c.* 1906.

242

243

244

243 C.R. Mackintosh – Stained oak chair with a rounded back designed for the Misses Cranston's Ingram Street tea-rooms, 1901.

244 C.R. Mackintosh – Oak chair and single ladder-back chair, designed for the Willow tea-rooms, 1904.

245 C.R. Mackintosh – Stained oak dining chair used by Mackintosh in his Mains Street flat, c. 1900.

246 C.R. Mackintosh – Stained oak chair designed for the Misses Cranston's Argyle Street tea-rooms, 1897.

245

246

247 C.R. Mackintosh – Interior of the
Willow tea-rooms, 1904.

248 C.R. Mackintosh – Hill House.
Main bedroom, 1903.

249

250

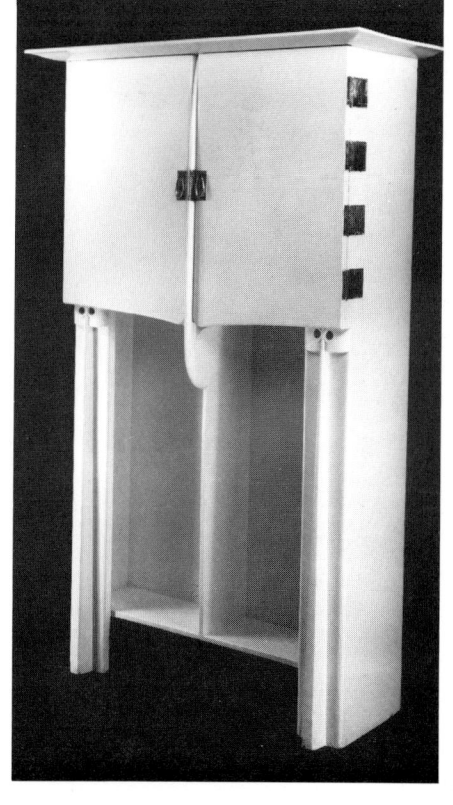

249 Interior of the C.R. Mackintosh
Memorial Exhibition, 1933.

250 C.R. Mackintosh – Brass
jewellery box, designed for Jessie
Keppie, *c.* 1895.

251 C.R. Mackintosh – Oak cabinet,
painted white, 1902.

251

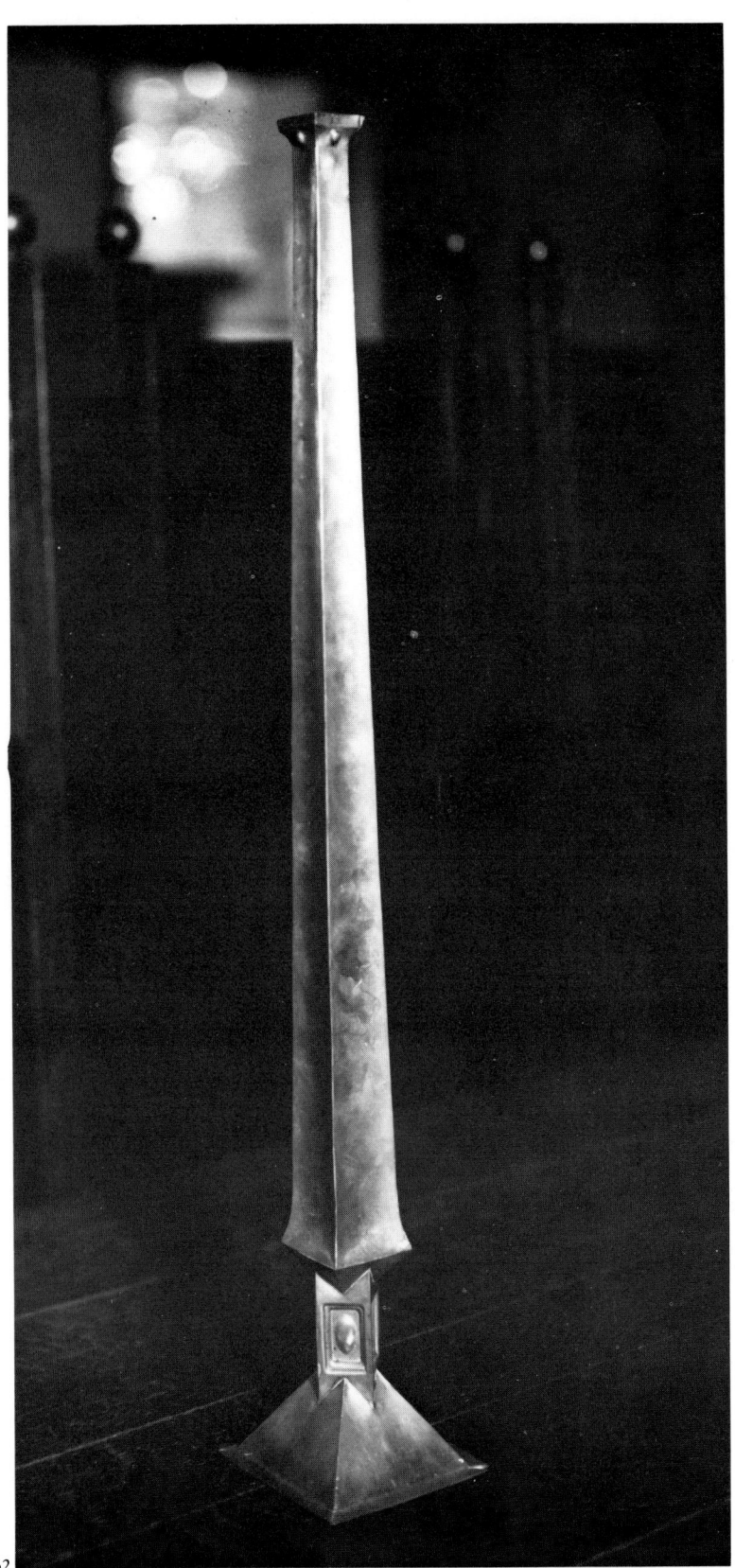

252

252 Frank Lloyd Wright – Copper vase, 'weed-holder', designed for Wright's library at Oak Park, *c.* 1893.

253 Frank Lloyd Wright – Oak armchair, designed for the Darwin R. Martin house in Buffalo, 1904.

254 Frank Lloyd Wright – Oak armchair, designed for the Ray W. Evans house in Beverly Hills, *c.* 1908.

255 Frank Lloyd Wright – Oak side chair, designed for the Isabel Roberts' house, 1908.

256 Frank Lloyd Wright – Oak side chair with dark brown stain finish, made for Francis Little's 'Northome', 1912-14.

253

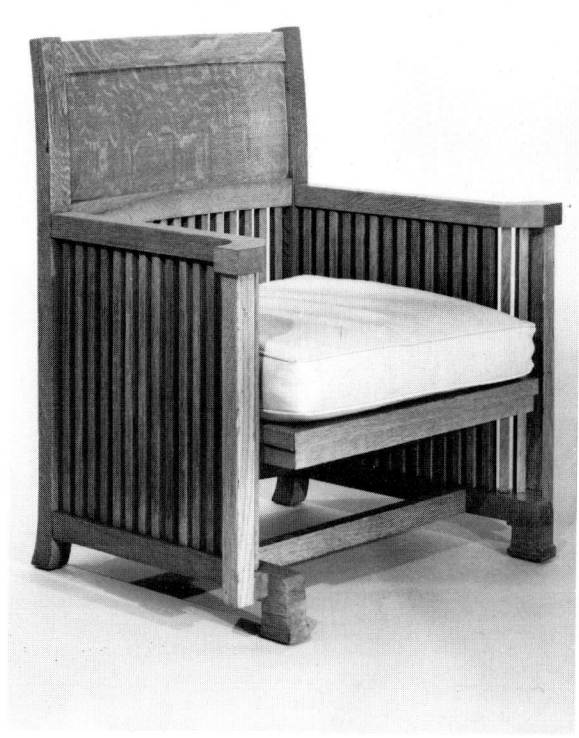

254

255

256

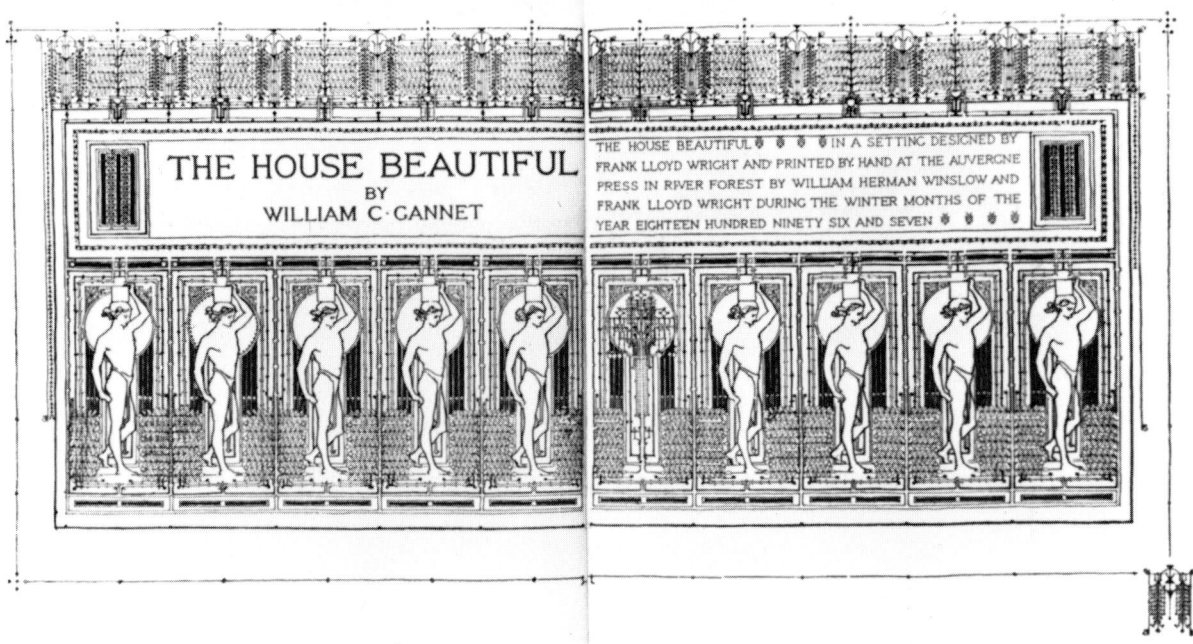

257

258

259

GEORGE · WALTON · AND · COMPANY · L^{TD}
DECORATORS; GLASS·STAINERS·AND· CABINET MAKERS
150·AND·152·WELLINGTON·STREET·
GLASGOW·
LONDON·ADDRESS·
GEORGE·WALTON·
STUDIO·16·WESTBOURNE·PARK·ROAD·
·BAYSWATER·LONDON·W
ESTABLISHED·1888·   ·TELEPHONE·N°274·

260

257 Frank Lloyd Wright – Title-page spread designed for *The House Beautiful* by William C. Gannet, 1896.

258 Frank Lloyd Wright – Oak gate-leg table with dark brown stain finish, made for Francis Little's 'Northome', 1912-14.

259 J.H. MacNair — The Kanthack medal, University of Liverpool, bronze, 1900.

260 George Walton – Letterhead, 1900.

261 George Walton – Armchair in stained oak with rush seat, *c.* 1896.

261

262 George Walton – Interior, Buchanan Street tea-rooms, designed for the Misses Cranston, 1895.

263 George Walton – Silk hanging, possibly designed for Alexander Morton, *c.* 1895. Used in the Buchanan Street tea-rooms in Glasgow.

264 George Walton – Kodak's Brompton Road branch, opened 1900.

265

266

265 E.A. Taylor – Display cabinet with leaded glass door, *c.* 1900.

266 George Logan – Mahogany bookcase with carved and inlaid decoration, doors glazed with stained and leaded glass, designed for Wylie and Lockhead, *c.* 1904.

267 Jessie M. King – Photograph of a child's nursery exhibited at the Musée Galliera, *c.* 1912.

267

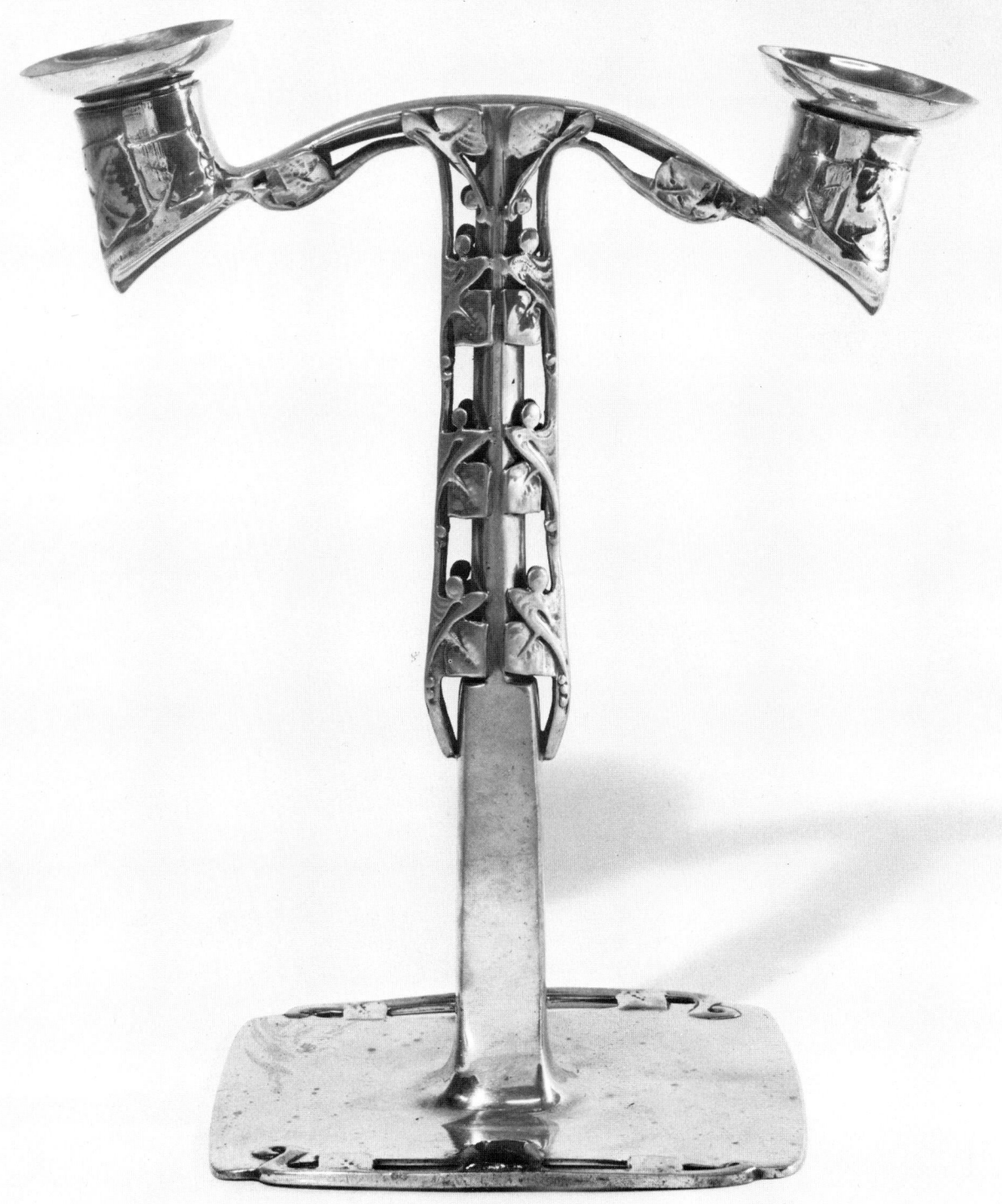

6 LIBERTY AND COMPANY

Arthur Lasenby Liberty, founder of Liberty and Co., was shrewd enough to see the potential of the craft ideal in commercial terms, and the security of his financial position, backed by a successful business, enabled him to secure designs from any artist or craftsman whom he admired. He rejected any idealistic concern with hand-craftsmanship and integrated the craftsman-designer with the established manufacturers, notably in the fields of wallpaper, textiles and metalwork, with the resulting benefits to the prices of the products.

Inevitably this plagiarism of the craft ideal reached a far larger public than the lovingly hand-crafted works of the guildsmen. In their success in introducing the public to new ideas in design there is an obvious similarity between Morris and Co. and Liberty's, with the significant difference that Morris insisted on the hand-making of things that would have been more suited to machine production. The wide success of the Liberty venture ensured that the public at large came to know the work of the Arts and Crafts designers, albeit in a modified form.

LIBERTY & COMPANY

Oriental warehouse and retail shop, Regent Street, London
Liberty & Co. was founded in 1875 by Arthur Lasenby Liberty (1843–1917). Formerly manager of Farmer and Rogers' Great Cloak and Shawl Emporium, Liberty conceived his shop in Regent Street as an oriental warehouse, dealing in oriental goods and fabrics, which he named East India House. With an enviable sense of timing that was to stand him in good stead in later ventures, Liberty found himself supplying the Japanese blue and white porcelain, the Indian silks and the oriental curious that were essential to the creation of the 'aesthetic' style, at that time the most fashionable manner for decoration. In 1884 a costume department was opened under the direction of E. W. Godwin, following quickly on the heels of the furnishing and decorating department, both departments designed to utilise the oriental silks which were a speciality of the firm. The furniture department also set out to provide furnishings, other than the oriental bric-à-brac which had been available with the other oriental goods, which would

268 Archibald Knox – Two-branched 'Tudric' pewter candlestick with enamel insets designed for Liberty and Co., 1905.

fit into the 'aesthetic' interior, and was under the direction of Leonard Wyburd until 1903. George Walton designed for Liberty's range of furniture and his elegant pieces are a welcome relief from Wyburd's massive designs, while the influence of Morris and Voysey is apparent in other designs. Richard Riemerschmid's elegant oak chair, designed in 1899, was used in the shop. The fabric department utilised the talents of a number of distinguished modern designers, including Léon Solon, Walter Crane, Arthur Silver, C. F. A. Voysey and Jessie M. King.

In the late nineties silverware and pewterware ventures were added to Liberty's already multifarious activities under the trade-names of 'Cymric' and 'Tudric' respectively. Liberty's registered their mark for silver and gold in 1894, but the first designs were produced late in 1898 or early 1899. The work was carried out by professional firms, the greater part of the objects being made by the Birmingham firm of W. H. Haseler, who also made the pewter. Here again in this department the talents of a number of distinguished designers, many of them involved with the Craft Revival Movement, were utilised, among them Archibald Knox, Arthur Gaskin, Jessie M. King, Rex Silver, Bernard Cuzner and Oliver Baker. At about the same date both Ann Macbeth and the Leek Embroidery Society (founded in about 1879 by the wife of Thomas Wardle who printed many of Liberty's fabrics) were designing for an embroidery department. Soon after this, in 1902, the carpet department was supplementing the original stock of Oriental and European carpets with specially made Donegal carpets, some designed by Archibald Knox and Mrs G. F. Watts.

Liberty's ventures into contemporary design were very successful, even providing an alternative name, *stile Liberty*, for the style known as Art Nouveau. However, their policy of strict anonymity for the artists made the exhibitions held by the Arts and Crafts Exhibition Society of paramount importance to the artists as well as ensuring that the personality of their most prolific and inventive designer, Archibald Knox, should remain in obscurity for half a century. Liberty's value to the Arts and Crafts Movement is equivocal since he disseminated a version of the style while diluting its impact. Ashbee believed that the 'Cymric' venture was largely responsible for the failure of the Guild of Handicraft, and the ethical basis for the Movement was entirely ignored, both in the methods of manufacture and in the shameless tampering with the original designs, but Liberty's were able, with their extremely competitive prices, to reach a vast public to whom the work of these designers would otherwise have remained unknown and unattainable.

English art pottery featured in Liberty catalogues at the turn of the century included work from a number of firms who were experimenting with hand-throwing, unusual glaze effects, sgraffito work and lustre decoration on their wares. These wares included the Bretby Art Pottery made by Henry

Tooth, who had worked with Christopher Dresser at John Harrison's Linthorpe Pottery, and William Ault, who established their pottery at Woodville, Derbyshire, in 1882; the Burmantofts Faience, an art pottery line introduced to supplement their established business in architectural terracotta work by Messrs Wilcox and Co., of Leeds in 1882; the Foley Pottery, made by Wileman & Co., of Longton in Staffordshire; the Barum Ware produced by C. H. Brannam at the Litchdon Street Pottery in Barnstable, Devon, from 1879; the Aller Vale Pottery, made by a firm in Newton Abbot, Devon, which formerly specialised in architectural wares, but started production of art pottery following a fire in 1881, recruiting the artists from the local art school; the Pilkington's Lancastrian Pottery made by the Pilkington Tile and Pottery Co., the Florian Ware made by William Moorcroft for James Mackintyre & Co., of Burslem in Staffordshire; the Della Robbia Pottery made by Harold Rathbone in Birkenhead; the Farnham Pottery, known at Liberty's as 'Green Ware' on account of the characteristic glaze made by A. Harris & Sons, at Farnham in Surrey, and the garden pottery with its Celtic-inspired decoration designed by Mrs Watts for the Compton Pottery at Guildford, Surrey.

Later Liberty's also stocked the wares of the Royal Doulton Pottery Co., Wedgwood & Co., and the Poole Pottery, all of whom had connections with craft revival artists and thus Liberty's can be seen as fulfilling a useful, even essential, entrepreneurial role in the Arts and Crafts Movement.

THE SILVER STUDIO

British design studio

The Silver Studio was founded by Arthur Silver (1853–1896), a fabric designer, and supplied Liberty's until the outbreak of the Second World War. The Silver Studio was responsible for some of Liberty's most characteristic and successful fabrics, including the famous 'Peacock Feather' which was revived to mark the centenary of the store in 1975. The reputation of 'Liberty Art Fabrics' on the continent was so great that the phrase *stile Liberty* was coined to describe the style otherwise known most commonly as Art Nouveau.

When Arthur Silver died in 1896 the running of the Studio was taken over by his young son Reginald (Rex) Silver (1879–1955) who had started to train as an artist, but who abandoned his studies in order to continue his father's work. Rex Silver designed silver for Liberty's 'Cymric' venture from the outset, the first designs dating from 1898, and already featuring the Celtic *entrelac* decoration that is the most recognisable characteristic of his work. This can be seen on the candlesticks illustrated here which were designed in about 1899. He also designed pieces in much the same style for the 'Tudric' pewter range, which was introduced by Liberty's in

269 Silver Studio – Jacquard woven furnishing fabric, 'Meuse' designed by Harry Napper for Liberty and Co., *c.* 1902.

1901, the designs being made up by the Birmingham firm W. H. Haseler, who also made up most of the silverwork and jewellery designs. During this period the Silver Studio contined to produce fabric designs, some by Harry Napper who worked for them at the beginning of the present century.

ARCHIBALD KNOX (1864–1933)

British designer and teacher

Born in the Isle of Man, Knox studied at Douglas School of Art, continuing to teach there, specialising in Celtic ornament. It is probable that between 1892 and 1896 he worked part-time in the architectural offices of M. H. Baillie Scott and it was probably through him that he came into contact with Liberty and Co. when he left the Isle of Man in 1897 for London, and took a teaching post at Redhill, Surrey. Liberty and Co. at this time were beginning to produce their first silver and metalwork and in 1899 the first 'Cymric' silverwork was produced, all handmade, with designs by Knox.

By 1900 he was their main designer and the inspiration behind their 'Celtic Revival', encouraged also by Liberty's Welsh managing director, John Llewellyn, though most of the designs were now for machine production. It is supposed that Knox worked in Christopher Dresser's studio and influences of his style can certainly be seen in some of Knox's work. In 1900 Knox returned to the Isle of Man, from where he submitted designs for Liberty's 'Tudric' pewter range. On his return to London in 1904 he both taught and designed for Liberty's, producing designs for silver, pewter, carpets, textiles, jewellery and pottery. In 1912, after his resignation from Kingston School of Art he left for Philadelphia and New York in the hope of new employment but returned unsuccessfully in 1913 to the Isle of Man where he continued to live until his death.

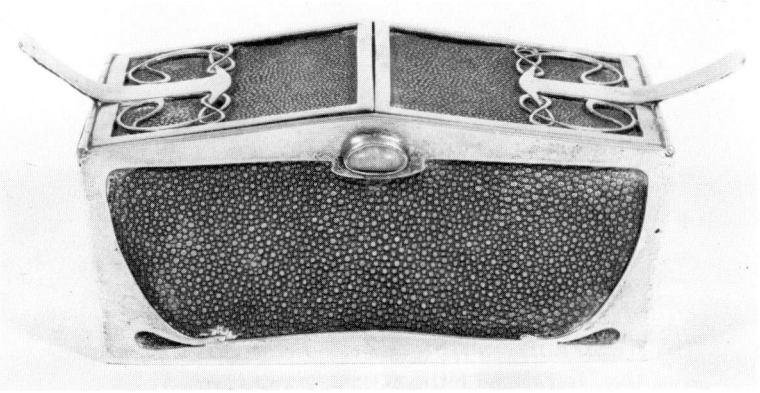

270 Archibald Knox (attrib.) – Silver and shagreen 'Cymric' cigarette box designed for Liberty and Co., 8½in. high, 1901.

Opposite
271 Archibald Knox – Silver biscuit box, with mother-of-pearl and enamel insets, 1901.

272

273

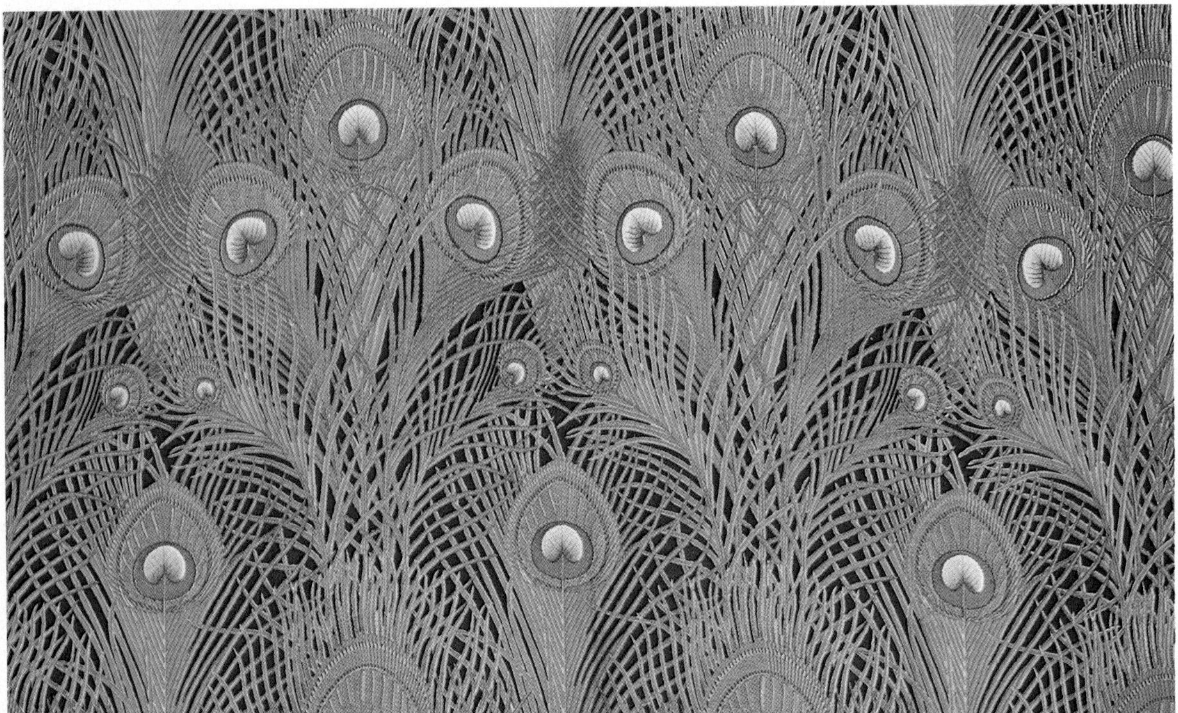

274

272 Liberty and Co. – Oak wash-stand inlaid with pewter, with a woven straw back panel, probably designed by Leonard F. Wyburd, *c.* 1899.

273 Liberty and Co. – Oak dressing-table inlaid with pewter, part of a bedroom suite probably designed by Leonard F. Wyburd, *c.* 1899.

274 Liberty and Co. – 'Peacock Feather'. Printed cotton designed by Arthur Silver, *c.* 1887.

275, 276 Liberty and Co. – Advertisements from the front and back covers of 'Modern Design in Jewellery and Fans', *The Studio*, special number, 1901.

275

276

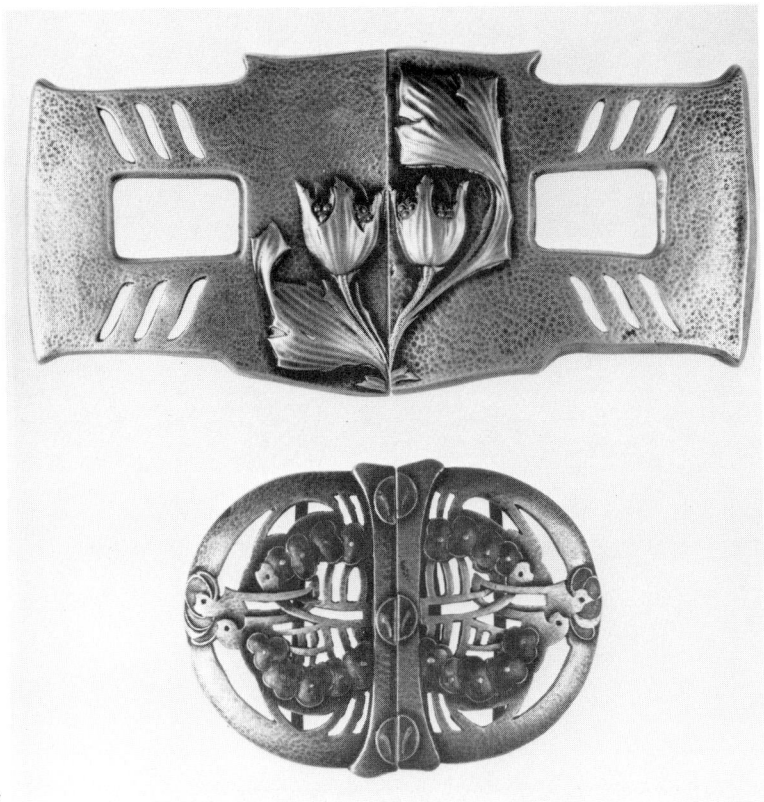

277

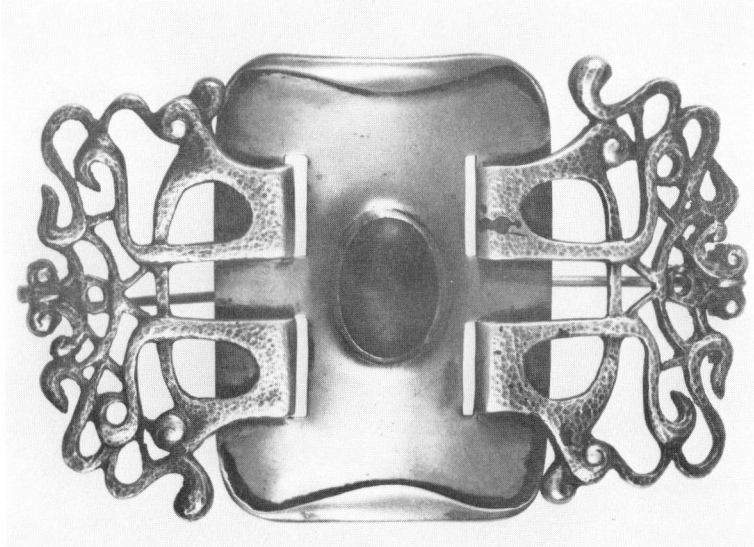

278

277 Liberty and Co. – 'Cymric' silver buckles; *(above)* 5in. width, 1902; *(below)* silver with enamel decoration, designed by Jessie M. King, 2⅞in. width, 1906.

278 Liberty and Co. – Silver belt buckle designed by Oliver Baker, 4½in. width, 1900.

279 Rex Silver (attrib.) – Silver and enamel 'Cymric' clock for Liberty and Co., 1903.

280 Liberty and Co. – Pewter clock with an enamelled face, c. 1905.

281 Liberty and Co. – Two 'Tudric' pewter clocks with enamelled decoration, 1903-4 and 1905.

282 Liberty and Co. – Silver clock with an enamelled face, 1918.

279

280

281

282

283

283 Archibald Knox – Hot-water jug in 'Tudric' pewter, designed for Liberty and Co., 1904.

284 Liberty and Co. – Covered box in 'Cymric' silver with repoussé and enamel decoration, 1903.

285 Archibald Knox (attrib.) – Green glass jug with silver bands, handle and lid, designed for Liberty and Co., c. 1903.

286 Rex Silver – 'The Conister'. Pair of silver candlesticks designed for Liberty and Co., 1899-1900.

287 Archibald Knox – Tea service, three pieces with a tray, in 'Tudric' pewter designed for Liberty and Co., 1903.

284

285

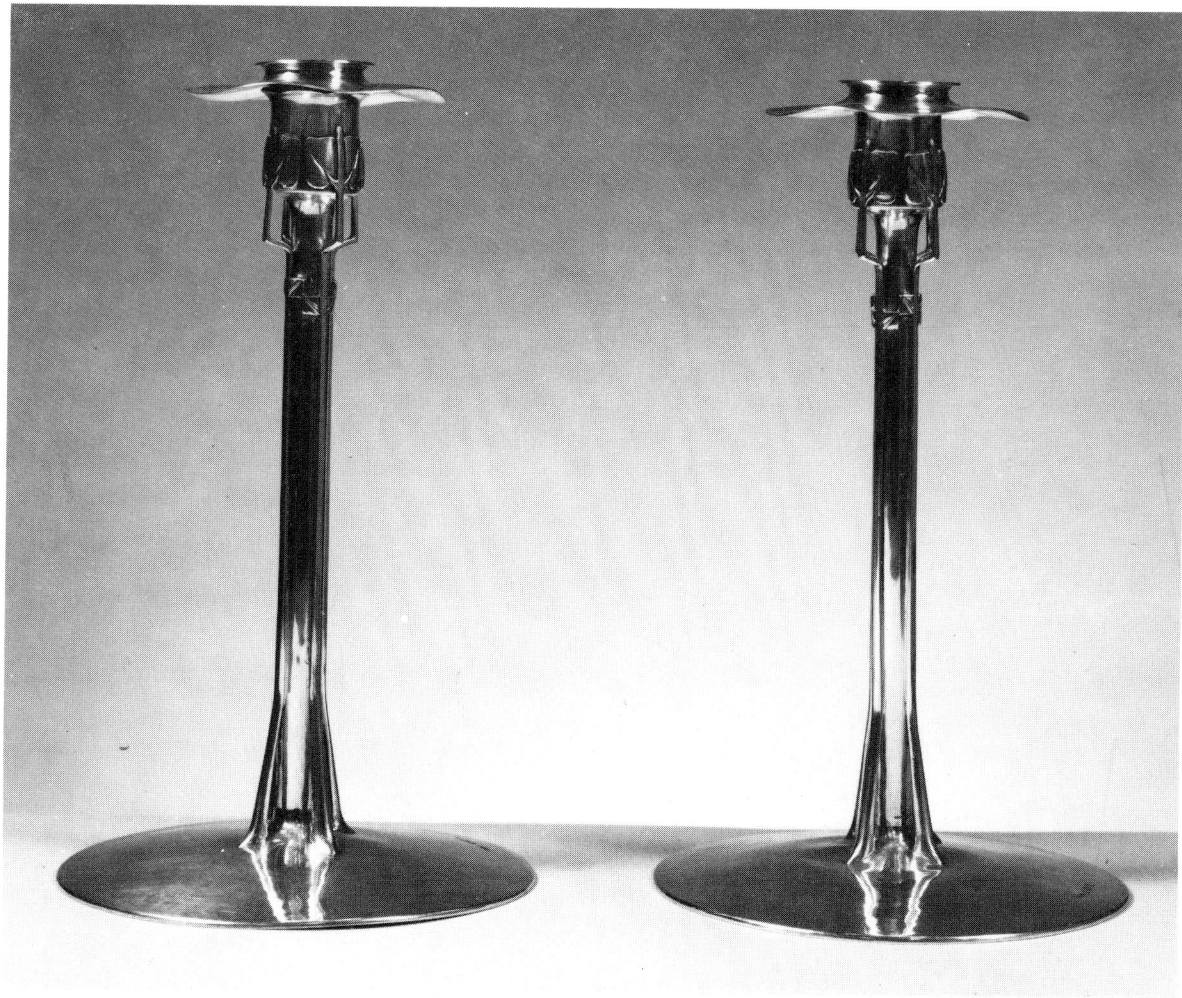

286

287

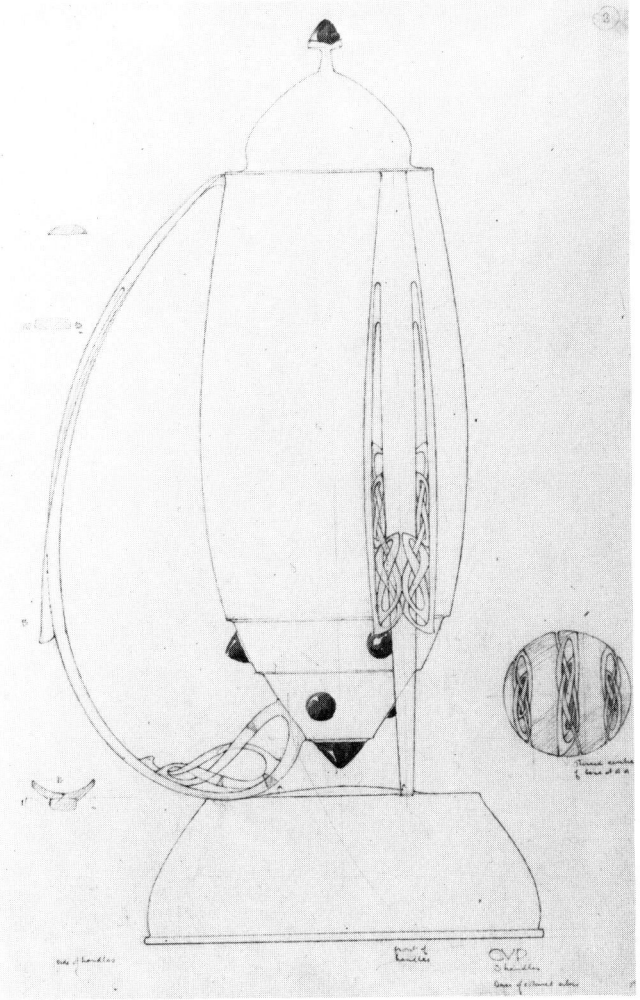

288

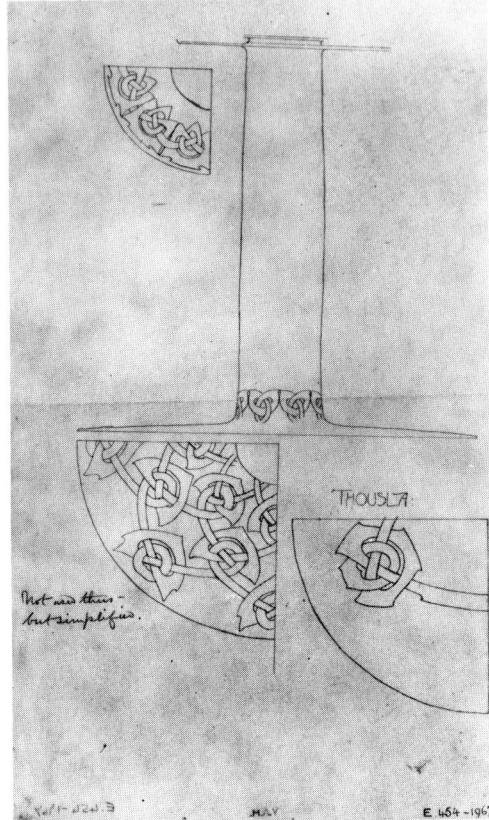

289

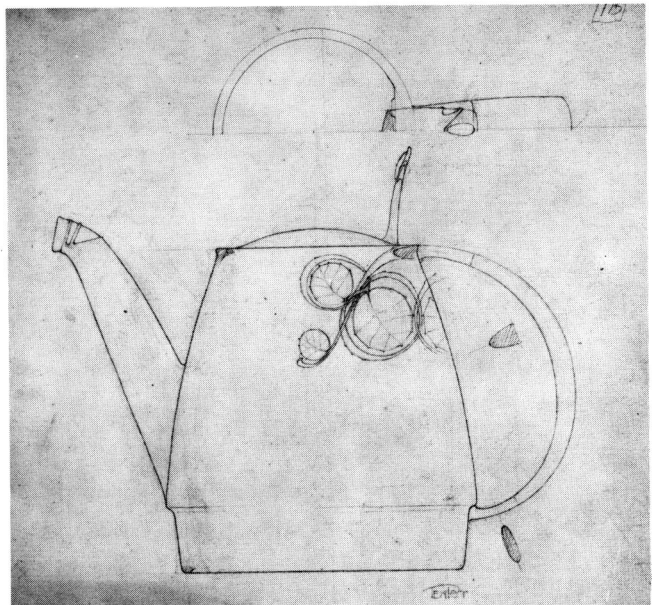

290

288 Archibald Knox – Design for a handled cup and cover, *c.* 1901.

289 Rex Silver – Design for a candlestick, *c.* 1900.

290 Archibald Knox – Design for a teapot, *c.* 1901.

291 George Walton – Walnut chair with inlaid decoration designed for Liberty and Co. and made at High Wickham by William Birch, *c.* 1899.

292 Liberty and Co. – Mahogany cabinet inlaid with stained woods, *c.* 1905.

293 Liberty and Co. – Cabinet with glazed doors and armchair in satinwood, part of a suite of furniture sold by Liberty's, possibly designed by George Walton, *c.* 1901.

291

292

293

294

295

294 Silver Studios – Woven silk and wool designed for Liberty and Co., 1895-1900.

295 Harry Napper – Printed cotton, made by G.P. and J. Baker, 1905.

Opposite
296 Charles Fleetwood Varley – Three boxes with decorative landscape enamels on the lids, made for Liberty and Co., 1900-1905: *(top)* Silver box; *(centre)* Pewter box; *(below)* Silver box.

Page 204
297 Liberty and Co. – Eight silver and enamel spoons, including 'Sarepta', 1899, and 'Medea', 1906; Silver knife, 1906; Silver and enamel stud box designed by Archibald Knox, *c.* 1903.

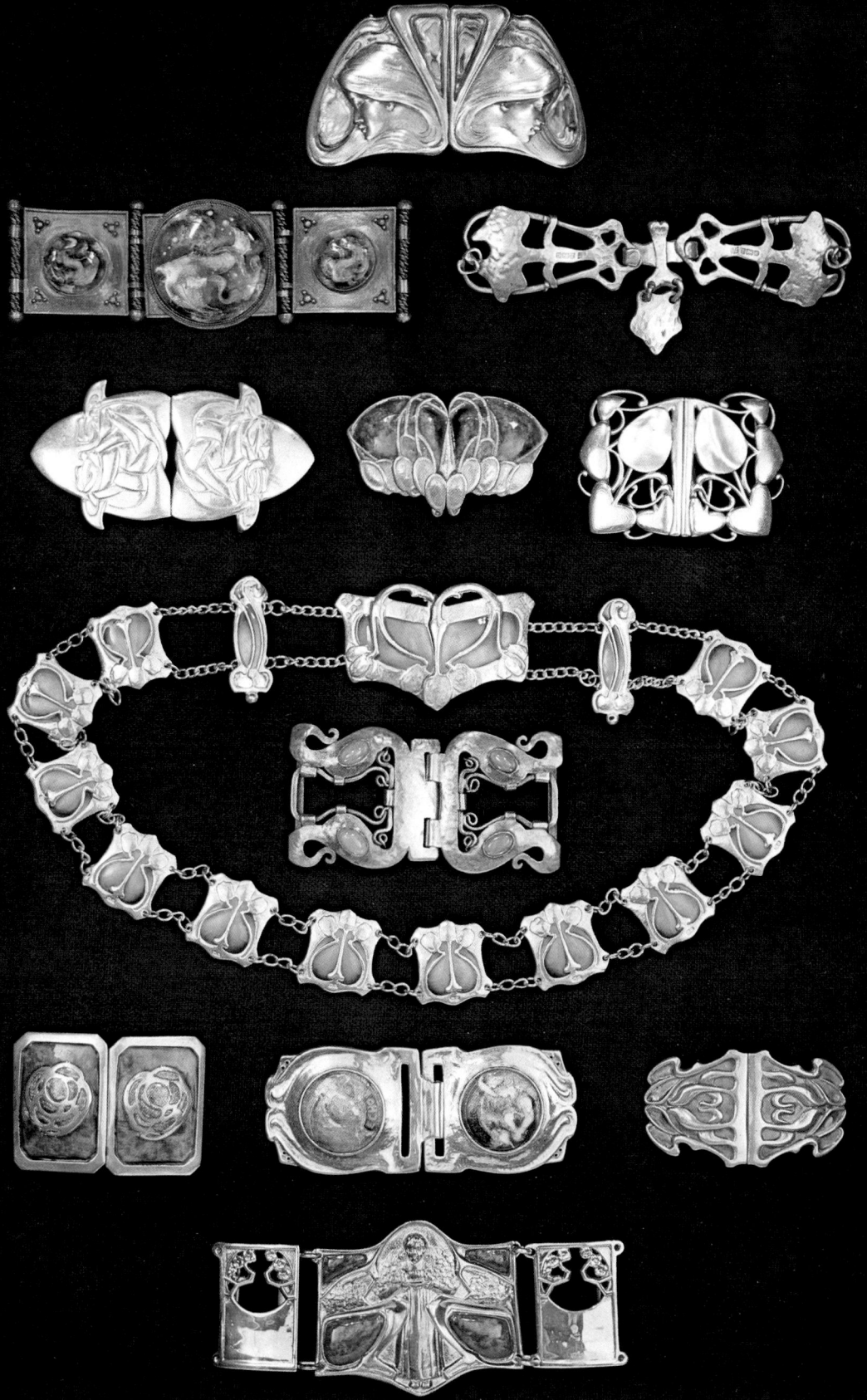

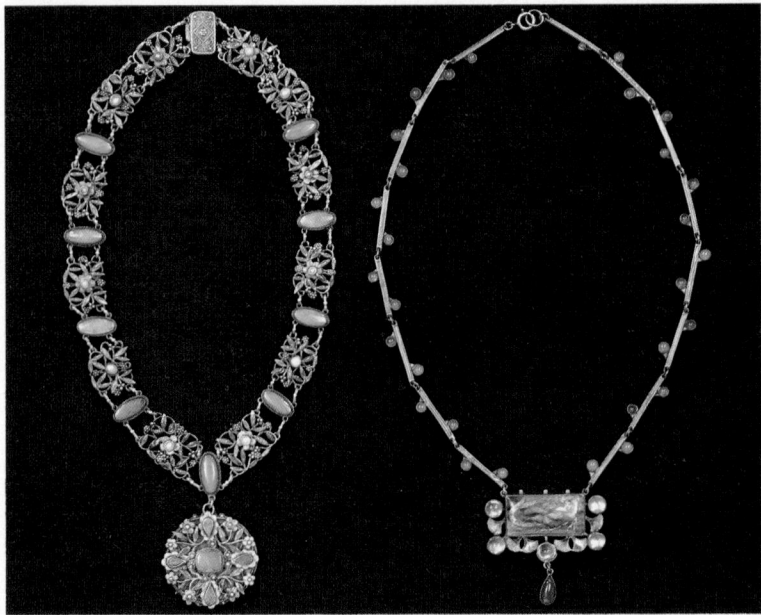

299

300 Arthur Gaskin – Silver and enamel
necklace set with opal and pearls, *c.*
1908 *(left)*; Fred Partridge – 'The
Mermaid', silver and enamel necklace
with crysophrases, *c.* 1905 *(right)*;
Partridge, a jeweller from Barnstable,
went to Chipping Campden with
Ashbee and he may also have designed
for Liberty and Co.

299 Archibald Knox – Silver casket on
a wooden carcass, set with a
heart-shaped opal matrix, made for
Liberty and Co., 1903.

Page 205

298 Group of silver buckles and clasps, 1900-1910: *(top)* Set with abalone shell, made by William Hutton; *(2nd row)* Silver and copper with enamels and a silver cloak clasp designed by Edgar Simpson, 1900; *(3rd row)* Three buckles by Liberty and Co., the left-hand one designed by Archibald Knox; *(4th row)* Belt and clasp in silver and enamel and a silver buckle set with oval cabochons designed by Oliver Baker for Liberty and Co.; *(5th row)* Silver and enamel waist clasps, 'Echo and Narcissus' designed and made by Gertrude Smith, *c.* 1900; *(6th row)* Silver and enamel belt plaque designed by Kate Harris for William Hutton.

301

301 Liberty and Co. – Silver vase set with cabochon turquoises, 1905.

302 Liberty and Co. – Silver hot-water jug, designed *c.* 1901.

302

7 THE EMERGENCE OF A 'POLYCHROMATIC' IDIOM

By the beginning of the twentieth century the split between ideal and style had finally become obvious. The work of Peter Waals, Ambrose Heal or Gordon Russell appeared to continue the craft tradition unbroken, but they were traditionalists from the outset. The true underlying significance of the movement led to the aesthetic path of influence being routed through an entirely different channel. The ideals which inspired Roger Fry's Omega Workshops or the 'Furniture Shop' of Arthur and Lucia Mathews, opened in San Francisco after the 1906 earthquake, still stemmed directly from Morris, but visually there is little to confirm this. When Roger Fry visited Ashbee in Chipping Campden to discuss the opening of the Omega, he found that though the ideals of the Guild of Handicraft still held good, the aesthetic had by then become irrelevant, remaining rooted in nineteenth century 'artistic' formula.

Ashbee himself disliked the work of the Omega, but it nevertheless provided a vital link connecting the ideals of Morris to the 'art for art's sake' of the Modern Movement. The pretence of corporate responsibility in a work of art was reluctantly dropped. From now on design was to be dominated by individuals, not least of whom was the towering figure of Frank Brangwyn, whose own first-hand experience of Morris's influence had not blinded him to the direction in which his art should go, and whose significance for decorative design in the present day is still incalculable.

SIR FRANK BRANGWYN, R.A. (1867–1956)

British painter, etcher, graphic artist and designer
Brangwyn, who was largely self-taught, was born in Bruges where his father, W. Curtis Brangwyn, the architect, ran an embroidery studio and workshop. His family returned to London in 1875 and he was educated at a day-school teaching himself to draw by copying at the Victoria and Albert Museum. There was insufficient money to send him to an art school, but he was befriended by Harold Rathbone and A. H. Mackmurdo, through whose influence he was able to get a job with Morris & Co., where he was employed in enlarging the designs for tapestries. He remained with Morris from 1882 to

303 Frank Brangwyn – 'Picking Gourds' window designed for Louis C. Tiffany, and exhibited at the Grosvenor Gallery in 1899.

1884. He exhibited for the first time at the Royal Academy in 1885, when he was barely eighteen years old.

After leaving Morris & Co. he travelled extensively, gathering material for his painting and graphic work in the East, in Africa and in Spain, still working for Morris in between his trips. In 1895 he assisted with the decorating of Samuel Bing's gallery in preparation for its transformation into the Maison de l'Art Nouveau, and also designed stained glass for Bing and for Tiffany in New York. He designed his first complete interior in 1900, for a house in South Kensington. Brangwyn was also allotted the task of decorating and furnishing the Biennale Exhibition held in Venice in 1905, and again in 1907. The furniture and panelling for the 1905 scheme was made to his design by the firm of J. S. Henry who, like Wylie and Lockhead in Glasgow, made a speciality of decorated furniture in the Art Nouveau style. Brangwyn's designs, in contrast, were of the starkest simplicity. He exhibited a range of 'cheap' furniture with the decorative panels which he executed for the exhibition at Ghent in 1913, again designed on the most simple lines.

During the whole of his mature years he worked on major decorative commissions including those for the Rockefeller Center in New York which he executed in collaboration with José Maria Sert and Diego Rivera. In 1919 he was elected a Royal Academician. He continued to design furniture, pottery, metalwork and jewellery, rugs, embroideries and fans, and to make elaborate and large-scale etchings. He was knighted in 1941.

DIRK VAN ERP (1860–1933)

American metalworker

Dick Van Erp was born in Leeuwarden, Holland, the son of the proprietor of a hardware shop and went to America in 1886. He worked in a naval shipyard and began to make vases out of brass shell casings. In 1908 he opened the Copper Shop in Oakland, moving in 1910 to San Francisco, where he went into partnership for a year with Miss D'Arcy Gaw. By 1915 the studio was flourishing, supported by his two children Agatha and William, making hand-crafted metalwork. Van Erp retired in 1929 but continued to design occasionally until his death.

CHARLES FLETCHER LUMMIS (fl. *c.* 1884–1910)

American writer

Lummis was educated at Harvard and became the City Editor of the Los Angeles *Times*. In 1895 he founded the California Landmarks Club with the aim of restoring the Missions. Throughout his life he supported the preservation and appreciation of Spanish, Mexican and Indian culture in California and he was the editor of *Land of Sunshine*, a magazine dedicated to the romantic revival of the finest aspects of the Spanish-Mexican past in a parallel manner to William Morris' mediaevalism.

ERNEST A. BATCHELDER (1875–1957)

American ceramist

Batchelder was born in New Hampshire and studied in Massachusetts and at the Birmingham School of Arts and Crafts in England. In 1901 he returned to America and attended the Harvard Summer School of Design where he was influenced by Denman W. Ross, one time President of the Boston Arts and Crafts Society. In 1904 he published *The Principles of Design* which advocated both Japanese and American Indian Art within its Arts and Crafts ethic. From 1904 to 1909 he taught, during the winters, at the Throop Polytechnic Institute — a liberal school which included practical arts — and, in summer, at the Minneapolis Guild of Handicrafts. In 1909 he set up his own school of Arts and Crafts in Pasadena. He is principally known for his tiles, influenced by Gothic design, which he admired on a second visit to England in 1905–6, and had contact with the Grueby Faience Company. He also contributed articles to *The Craftsman*.

304 Ernest A. Batchelder – Cast ceramic tile, 1909-20.

GREENE & GREENE

American architects and interior designers

Charles Sumner Greene and Henry Mathew Greene were born in 1868 and 1870 in Cincinnati, were educated in St. Louis and at the MIT and then worked for various architects in Boston. In 1893 they moved to Pasadena and began a small practice, designing mainly Georgian or Queen Anne style houses. In 1901 (and again in 1909) Charles visited England and Europe and absorbed the Arts and Crafts ideals. They were also influenced by Japanese design, through the 1893 World's Columbian Exposition in Chicago and through association with John Benz, an importer of oriental antiques.

Between 1907 and 1909 they designed their four great houses — for the Blackers, Gambles, Pratts and Maybecks — for which they also designed the gardens. Charles also designed most of the furniture. Ashbee visited them in 1909 and was impressed by the Gamble house. From 1907–15 their work was featured in *The Craftsman*. After 1910, however, their work won four large commissions and almost nine for furniture as well. In 1916 Charles left for Carmel, California and did not return. Their last work was in 1923 and the furniture was made by Peter Hall. Charles died in 1957.

305 Charles and Henry Sumner Greene – Leaded art glass ceiling lamp made for the Freeman Ford house, 1909.

THE RUSKIN POTTERY

British art pottery workshop

The Ruskin Pottery was started in 1898 by W. Howson Taylor, son of the remarkable headmaster of the Birmingham School of Art, E. R. Taylor, who was himself a friend of Morris and Burne-Jones and a pioneer in the teaching of craft skills combined with fine art. Edward Taylor provided some of the decorative designs for the Ruskin Pottery, but W. H. Taylor was chiefly interested in glaze effects, and most of his pots are made in simple oriental shapes, their only decoration being the random staining of the coloured glazes.

His experiments included working with high temperatures to produce his famous 'high-fired' effects, and he mastered the difficult techniques of 'soufflé' glaze, lustre glaze and 'flambé' glaze. His obsession with glaze techniques is comparable with that of the Robertsons at the Chelsea pottery in America, and his work is similar in conception to that of Bernard Moore in England, all of them searching for the ways to reproduce the intense glaze colours found in Chinese ceramics. The pottery at West Smethwick continued until 1935, closing only two months before W. H. Taylor's death.

UNIVERSITY CITY POTTERY

American pottery college

In 1907 Edward Gardner Lewis, an entrepreneur and patron of arts and education, founded the American Women's league for the creation of better opportunities for women. In 1903 porcelain clay was found in University City and Lewis opened a pottery at his Art Institute in St. Louis in 1909. He persuaded Taxile Doat to leave Sèvres and come to University City, along with Mrs Adelaide Alsop Robineau, her husband Samuel who had translated Doat's work, and Frederick H. Rhead, an Englishman who had worked for S. A. Weller (1902–4) and the Roseville Pottery Co., Ohio (1904–8). Kathryn E. Cherry also came from St. Louis to teach at University City.

Thousands undertook correspondence courses and exceptional students were invited to study for one year, instructed by the masters at the Institute. By 1911 Lewis' empire was failing and he was investigated for mail fraud. All but Taxile Doat and his two French associates left. The American Women's League had already failed in 1910. The pottery continued until 1914 and Doat returned, disillusioned, to France in 1915. Some of the finest American pottery was made there and Mrs Robineau's work won the Grand Prix at the Turin International Exhibition in 1911.

ADELAIDE ALSOP ROBINEAU (1865–1929)

American ceramist

Born in Connecticut, she taught china painting and exhibited as a water-colourist and miniaturist. In 1899 she married her French-born husband Samuel and began to edit the *Keramic Studio* in Syracuse — an attempt to educate people in good design for pottery. In 1903 she began experimenting with porcelain and crystalline glazes, championing conventionalised Beaux-Arts designs. From 1909 to 1911 she worked with Taxile Doat, the celebrated potter from the Sèvres Manufactory, and in 1911 won the Grand Prix at the International Exhibition of Decorative Arts at Turin for her *Scarab Vase*, made at the University City Pottery. The work produced there was sophisticated, high-fired porcelain with flambé and crystalline glazes, perhaps unrivalled in America at that time.

MARBLEHEAD POTTERY

American art pottery company

Begun in 1905 as part of Dr. Herbert J. Hall's programme of therapy for nervous patients. He engaged Arthur E. Baggs as a technician. The pottery was made a separate entity and its wares first offered to the public in 1908. Matt glazes with conventionalised designs were used. The idea of linking pottery production to social needs was also practised at the Paul Revere Pottery, Boston and Frederick Rhead's Arequipa Pottery in California.

306 Frederick H. Rhead – Ceramic pot made at Santa Barbara, 1913-16.

FULPER POTTERY COMPANY

American art pottery company

The Fulper Pottery Company was established in 1805 and was the oldest pottery in the United States. In 1910 they introduced an art pottery line, influenced by Chinese shapes and glazes, known as 'Vase-Kraft' and also began to produce pottery lamps — 'Art pottery put to practical uses'. An endless variety of shapes and glazes — 'Mirror Glaze', 'Mission Matte', 'Leopard Skin', etc. — were produced. Fulper won first prize in ceramics at the Panama-Pacific International Exposition, San Francisco 1915. The factory closed in 1929.

A. F. & L. K. MATHEWS

American artists and interior designers

Arthur F. Mathews (1860–1945) was born in Wisconsin and moved to California in 1866, settling in Oakland in 1867. From

307 Arthur and Lucia Mathews – Cabinet and boxes for the Furniture Shop in San Francisco, 1906-20.

1875 to 1879 he worked as an architectural draughtsman in his father's office. From 1881 to 1884 he worked as a designer and illustrator and the period between 1885 and 1889 was spent in Paris studying painting at the Académie Julian under Boulanger and Lefebre where he exhibited three years running at the Paris Salon. He joined the Californian School of Design in 1889 and was Director of the School from 1890 to 1906.

In 1894 he married his pupil Lucia Kleinhans (1870–1955) who was born in San Francisco and who had studied, from 1893, at the Mark Hopkins Institute of Art. They visited Paris together in 1898 where Lucia attended Whistler's Académie Carmen. After the Great Fire of 1906 they designed and moved into 1717 California Street where they started the Philopolis Press and Furniture Shop, employing thirty to fifty craftsmen for their larger interior schemes. Lucia did much of the inlay and painting work on the furniture. Arthur is famous mostly for his murals and was a painter-decorator rather than artist-craftsman. The Furniture Shop ceased production in 1920; the last issue of *Philopolis* was in September 1916.

OMEGA WORKSHOPS (1913–1919)

British decorative art workshops

The Omega Workshops opened at 33 Fitzroy Square in Bloomsbury in July 1913 under the direction of Roger Fry (1866–1934), artist, critic and writer and one-time curator of paintings at the Metropolitan Museum of Art in New York. Fry was a life-long friend of C. R. Ashbee, whom he had met at Cambridge. He was also the organiser of the famous exhibition of Post-Impressionist pictures at the Grafton Galleries in 1910, which introduced the public to the work of Cézanne, van Gogh and their circle, still entirely unknown in England at that time. The idea for the Omega Workshops grew out of Fry's preoccupation with the revival of mural decoration. In 1901 Fry had undertaken the decoration of the students' dining-room at the Borough Polytechnic, assisted by Duncan Grant, Frederick Etchells and Bernard Adeney. In 1912, together with Duncan Grant and Vanessa Bell (1879–1961), he had started to paint large frescoes in his own house 'Durbins' at Guildford, which he had designed himself and built in 1909.

At an exhibition of the Grafton Galleries Group in March 1913, which was held at the Alpine Club Gallery, Fry had already included some examples of furniture which he and his circle were decorating, and the aim of the Omega Workshop company was to demonstrate the desirability of having items in every day use designed and decorated by artists, especially within the field of Post-Impressionism as well as to provide employment for artists. His ambition was to undertake the decoration of a complete interior. He was fortunate in securing such a commission for the Workshop in 1914, for Henry Harris's house in Bedford Square, which was carried out in collaboration with Duncan Grant and Vanessa Bell. In spite of a satisfactory number of commissions including the decorating of a scheme to be shown at the Ideal Home Exhibition in 1915 (over which — through a misunderstanding — Fry quarrelled irrevocably with Wyndham Lewis, and also Etchells and Edward Wadsworth, all of whom had worked for him at the Workshop) and the showing of work at the Arts and Crafts Exhibition at the Royal Academy in 1916, the development of such an experimental decorating firm was badly hampered by the outbreak of the First World War only a year after it had opened.

The Workshops survived in a financially insecure state throughout the war, adding various other activities to the main business of wall painting, furniture design and decoration, surviving competition from Heal's in Tottenham Court Road. The actual furniture making was contracted out to craftsmen, or second-hand furniture painted by the artists. These activities included pottery (editions of Fry's models were carried out by the Poole Pottery), fabrics, needlework and publishing, and the establishment of the Evening Club which was rendered acutely uncomfortable by the lack of chairs, the visitors to these gatherings being expected to sit on canvas floor cushions (a foretaste of future fashion as in so much else in the 'Omega' style). At last in June 1919 the Workshops were closed and in 1920 the Company went into voluntary liquidation. Duncan Grant and Vanessa Bell continued to add decorative schemes to their work as painters for many years.

308 Charles Sumner Greene – Card table and chairs made for the Blacker house, 1909.

309 M. H. Baillie Scott –
Writing cabinet with incised and
coloured decoration on ebonized
wood and inset beaten pewter panels
depicting the serpent in the Garden of
Eden. It is inscribed below the
fall-front, *Litera: Scripta: Manet.*

310 Arthur and Lucia Mathews –
Mahogany and brass writing table,
with stained and incised
polychromatic decoration, made for
the Furniture Shop, *c.* 1908.

310

215

311

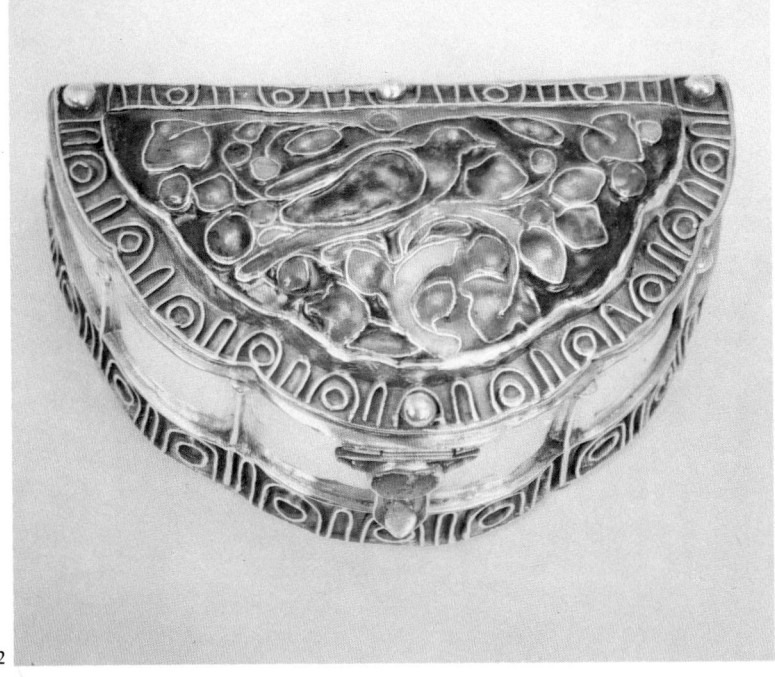

312

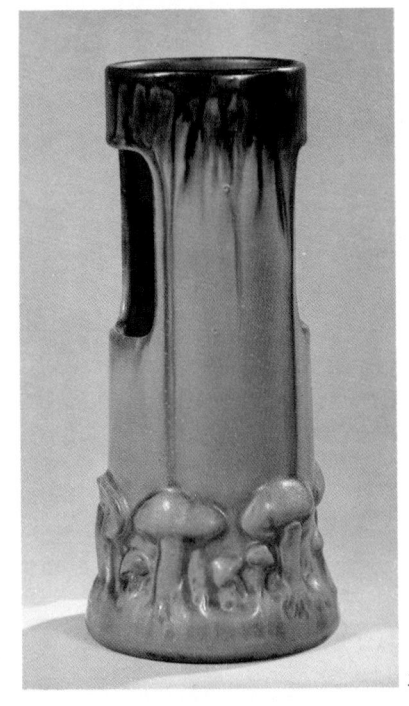

313

311 *(left)* Della Robbia Pottery – Griffon-handled vase with painted base with sgraffito decoration, 1901; *(right)* A. Harris and Sons, Farnham – Two-handled 'greenware' vase with sgraffito decoration of stylized foliage, *c.* 1900.

312 Elizabeth E. Copeland – Silver and enamel casket.

313 Fulper Pottery Co. – 'Mushroom' vase from the 'Vase-Kraft' line, 1910-14.

314 Frank Brangwyn – Cabinet and stand in cherry wood decorated with carved and coloured gesso, made by Paul Turpin, *c.* 1910.

315 Frank Brangwyn – Scheme for a room with mural decoration for the Venice Exhibition of 1905. Illustrated in *The Studio*, Vol. 34, 1905, p.284.

316

317

318

319

316 Dick Van Erp – Hammered copper lamp, shade with mica inserts, c. 1912.

317 Ernest A. Batchelder – Cast ceramic tiles, 1909-12.

318 Ernest A. Batchelder – Cast ceramic garden pot, 1912.

319 Ernest A. Batchelder – Cast ceramic tile, 1909-20.

320 Charles Sumner Greene – Mahogany table and chairs with leather seats, made for the Robinson house, 1906.

321 Charles Sumner Greene – Teak storage bench made for the Blacker house, 1909.

320

321

322

323

322 Charles Sumner Greene – Teak chest made for the Blacker house, 1909.

323 Charles Sumner Greene – Armchair made for the Blacker house, 1909.

324 Adelaide Alsop Robineau – the 'Viking Ship' case. Porcelain vase with relief decoration, 7¼ in. high, 1908.

325 University City Pottery – Two vases with crystalline glazes designed by Taxile Doat, c. 1910.

326 Frederick H. Rhead – Panel of ceramic tiles for garden use, made at the Santa Barbara pottery, 1913-16.

324

325

326

327

329

327 Ruskin Pottery – Group of wares with high-fired and other glaze effects, 1910-18.

328 Marblehead Pottery – Painted pottery vase with matt glazes, 7in. high, 1908-10.

329 Fulper Pottery Co. – Pottery vase with a green crystalline glaze, 6⅞in. high, c. 1910.

330 Arthur and Lucia Mathews – Group of furniture and decorative items for the Furniture Shop in San Francisco, 1906-20.

328

330

331

331 *Philopolis* magazine, edited by Arthur Mathews, 1909.

332 Lucia Mathews – Painted box for the Furniture Shop in San Francisco, *c.* 1908.

333 Omega Workshops – Pair of painted armchairs, *c.* 1913.

334 Omega Workshops – Round table with painted decoration by Roger Fry, 1913-19.

332

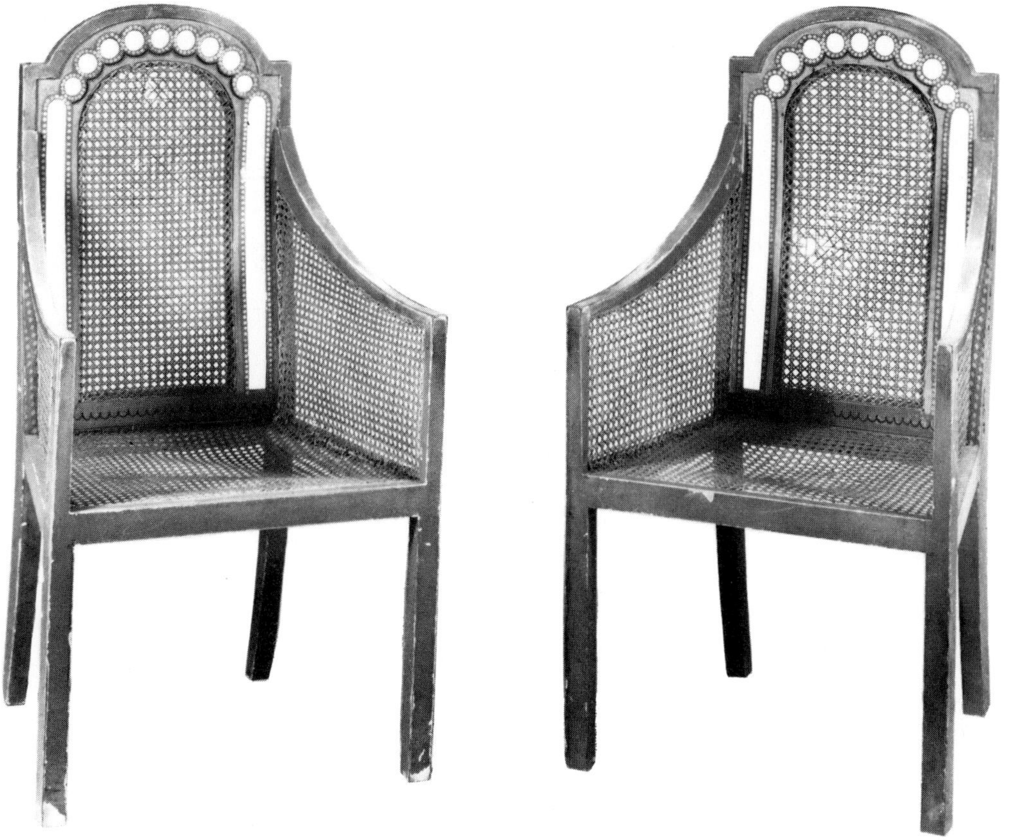

333

334

BIBLIOGRAPHY

BOOKS

Adburgham, Alison *Liberty's: A Biography of a Shop*, London 1975.

Arnold, Matthew *Culture and Anarchy*, London 1869.

Arts and Crafts Essays, by members of the Arts and Crafts Exhibition Society, London 1893.

Ashbee, C. R. *Craftsmanship in a Competitive Industry*, London 1908.

Ashbee, C. R. *Modern English Silverwork*, London 1909, new edition with introductory essays by Alan Crawford and Shirley Bury, London 1974.

Ashbee, C. R. *The Guild of Handicraft*, memoirs, London 1909.

Aslin, Elizabeth, *Nineteenth Century English Furniture*, London 1962.

Aslin, Elizabeth *The Aesthetic Movement, prelude to Art Nouveau*, London 1969.

Banham, Reyner *Theory and Design in the First Machine Age*, London 1960.

Bell, Quentin *The Schools of Design*, London 1963.

Benson, W. A. S. *Elements of Handicraft and Design*, London 1893.

Bing, Samuel *La Culture Artistique en Amérique*, Paris 1896.

Blomfield, Sir Reginald *Richard Norman Shaw*, London 1940.

Bøe, Alf *From Gothic Revival to Functional Form*, Oslo 1957.

Bolsterli, Margaret J. *The Early Community at Bedford Park*, London 1977.

Briggs, Asa *William Morris, Selected Writings and Designs*, Harmondsworth 1962.

Brooks, H. Allen *The Prairie School: Frank Lloyd Wright and his Midwest Contemporaries*, Toronto 1972.

Burne-Jones, Georgiana *Memorials of Edward Burne-Jones*, 2 vols., London 1904.

Carlyle, Thomas *Past and Present*, London 1843.

Carlyle, Thomas *Heroes and Hero-Worship*, London 1841.

Cobden-Sanderson, T. *The Arts and Crafts Movement*, London 1905.

Cole, Sir Henry *Fifty Years of Public Work*, 2 vols., London 1884.

Crane, Walter *The Claims of Decorative Art*, London 1892.

Crane, Walter *The Bases of Design*, London 1898.

Crane, Walter *Line and Form*, London 1900.

Crane, Walter *An Artist's Reminiscences*, London 1907.

Crane, Walter *William Morris to Whistler*, London 1911.

Day, Lewis F. *Everyday Art: Short Essays on the Arts Not-fine*, 1882.

Day, Lewis F. *The Anatomy of Pattern*, London 1887.

Day, Lewis F. *The Planning of Ornament*, London 1888.

Dresser, Dr. Christopher *The Art of Decorative Design*, London 1862.

Dresser, Dr. Christopher *Principles of Decorative Design*, London 1873.

Dresser, Dr. Christopher *Studies in Design*, London 1876.

Dresser, Dr. Christopher *Principles of Art*, London 1881.

Eastlake, Charles L. *Hints on Household Taste in Furniture*, London 1868.

Engels, Friedrich *Condition of the Working-Class in England in 1884*, London 1892.

Evans, Paul F. *Art Pottery of the United States*, New York 1974.

Fitzgerald, Penelope *Edward Burne-Jones, a Biography*, London 1975.

Furst, Herbert *The Decorative Art of Frank Brangwyn*, London 1924.

Gaunt, William S. and M. D. E. Clayton Stamm *William De Morgan*, London 1971.

Girouard, Mark *Sweetness and Light*, London 1977.

Greeves, T. A. *Bedford Park, the first Garden Suburb*, London 1975.

Henderson, Philip *William Morris, his Life, Work and Friends*, London 1967.

Houghton, Walter E. *The Victorian Frame of Mind*, Yale 1957.

Howarth, Thomas *Charles Rennie Mackintosh and the Modern Movement*, London 1952, new edition 1977.

Hubbard, Elbert *Elbert Hubbard's Scrapbook*, New York 1923.

Jewson, Norman *By Chance I did Rove*, Warwick 1973.

Jones, Owen *The Grammar of Ornament*, London 1856.

Klingender, F. D. *Art and the Industrial Revolution*, London 1968.

Koch, Robert *Louis C. Tiffany, Rebel in Glass*, New York 1974.

Kornwolf, James D. *M. H. Baillie Scott and the Arts and Crafts Movement*, Baltimore and London 1972.

Lectures on the Great Exhibition of 1851, Society of Arts, 1852/3.

Lethaby, W. R. *Architecture, Mysticism and Myth*, London 1892, facsimile reprints London 1974, New York 1975.

Lethaby, W. R. *Morris as Work-Master*, London 1902.

Lethaby, W. R. *Philip Webb and his Work*, Oxford 1935.

Lethaby, W. R. and others, *Ernest Gimson, His Life and Work*, Stratford-on-Avon 1924.

Lindsay, Jack *William Morris*, London 1975.

MacCarthy, Fiona *All Things Bright and Beautiful, Design in Britain, 1830 to Today*, London 1972.

Mackail, J. W. *The Life of William Morris*, 2 vols., London 1899.

Macleod, Robert *Charles Rennie Mackintosh*, London 1968.

Massé, H. J. L. J. *The Art Worker's Guild, 1884–1934*, Oxford 1935.

Mayhew, Henry *London Labour and the London Poor*, London 1851.

Morris, May (ed.) *The Collected Works of William Morris*, 24 vols., London 1910–14.

Morris, William *Architecture, Industry and Wealth*, collected papers, lectures and articles on pattern design, textiles, craftsmanship, architecture and the relationship of art and socialism, London 1902.

Mortimer, Raymond and Dorothy Todd, *The New Interior Decoration*, London 1929.

Naylor, Gillian *The Arts and Crafts Movement*, London 1971.

Pater, Walter *Studies in the History of the Renaissance*, London 1873.

Pater, Walter *Plato and Platonism*, London 1893.

Pevsner, Nikolaus *Pioneers of the Modern Movement, from William Morris to Walter Gropius*, London 1936.

Pevsner, Nikolaus *Sources of Modern Architecture and Design*, London 1968.

Pevsner, Nikolaus *Studies in Art, Architecture and Design*, Vol. 2, London 1968.

Pevsner, Nikolaus (ed.) *The Anti-Rationalists*, London 1973.

Pugin, A. W. *Contrasts: or a Parallel between the Noble Edifices of the Middle Ages and the corresponding Buildings of the Present Day: showing the Present Decay of Taste*, London 1836.

Pugin, A. W. *The True Principles of Pointed or Christian Architecture*, London 1841.

Read, Sir Herbert *Art and Industry*, London 1934.

Ruskin, John *The Collected Works*, ed. Cook and Wedderburn, London 1903–12.

Russell, Sir Gordon *Designer's Trade*, London 1968.

Saint, Andrew *Richard Norman Shaw*, Yale 1976.

Schaeffer, Herwin *The Roots of Modern Design*, London 1970.

Scully, Vincent J. Jr. *The Shingle Style: Architectural Theory and Design from Richardson to the Origins of Wright*, New Haven and London, 1955.

Sedding, J. D. *Art and Handicraft*, London 1893.

Service, Alistair (ed.) *Edwardian Architecture and its Origins*, London 1975. A selection of articles written between 1897 and 1975, including sections on *Arts and Crafts Architecture* and *Scotland at the Turn of the Century*.

Shaw-Sparrow, Walter *Frank Brangwyn and his Work*, London 1910.

Spencer, Isobel *Walter Crane*, London 1975.

Stirling, A. M. W. *William De Morgan and his Wife*, London 1922.

Sutton, Denys (ed.) *The Letters of Roger Fry*, London 1972.

Thomson, Paul *The Work of William Morris*, London 1967.

Tilbrook, A. J. *The Designs of Archibald Knox for Liberty and Co.*, London 1976.

Triggs, Oscar Lovell *Chapters in the History of the Arts and Crafts Movement*, Chicago 1902.

Veblen, Thorstein *The Theory of the Leisure Class*, London 1899.

Wakefield, Hugh *Victorian Pottery*, London 1962.

Watkin, David *Morality and Architecture*, Oxford 1977.

Watkinson, Raymond *William Morris as a Designer*, London 1967.

Watkinson, Raymond *Pre-Raphaelite Art and Design*, London 1970.

Weir, Robert W. S. *William Richard Lethaby*, London 1932.

Wilde, Oscar, *Art and Decoration: Being Extracts from Reviews and Miscellanies*, London 1920.

Williams, Raymond *Culture and Society, 1780–1950*, London 1958.

Wilson, Henry *Silverwork and Jewellery*, London 1903.

Wright, Frank Lloyd *A Testament*, New York n.d.

CATALOGUES

Andersen, Moore and Winter *California Design: 1910*, exhibition catalogue, California 1974.

Birmingham Gold and Silver 1773–1973, exhibition catalogue, Birmingham City Museum and Art Gallery, 1973.

Charles Rennie Mackintosh 1868–1928: Architecture, Design and Painting, exhibition catalogue, Royal Scottish Museum, Edinburgh, 1969.

Clark, Robert Judson (ed.) *The Arts and Crafts Movement in America 1876–1916*, exhibition catalogue, Princeton 1972.

Ernest Gimson, exhibition catalogue, Leicester Museums and Art Gallery, 1969.

Janson, Dora Jane *From Slave to Siren*, exhibition catalogue, Duke Museum of Art, North Carolina 1972.

Jessie M. King and E. A. Taylor, sale catalogue, Sotheby's, London 1977.

Jewellery and Jewellery Design 1850–1930, and John Paul Cooper 1869–1933, exhibition catalogue, The Fine Art Society, London 1975.

Liberty's: 1875–1975, exhibition catalogue, Victoria and Albert Museum, London 1975.

Mathews: Masterpieces of the California Decorative Style, exhibition catalogue, Oakland Museum, California 1972.

Official Descriptive and Illustrative Catalogue, The Great Exhibition 1851.

Philadelphia Centennial Exposition Catalogue, 1876.

Reports of the Juries, The Great Exhibition 1851.

The Arts and Crafts Movement 1890–1930, exhibition catalogue, Fine Art Society, London 1973.

The Art Journal Illustrated Catalogue, The Great Exhibition 1851.

The Earthly Paradise, exhibition catalogue of the work of the Birmingham Group, The Fine Art Society, London 1969.

The Shakers, exhibition catalogue, Victoria and Albert Museum, London 1975.

Victorian and Edwardian Decorative Arts, exhibition catalogue, Victoria and Albert Museum, London 1952.

Victorian and Edwardian Decorative Art: The Handley-Read Collection, exhibition catalogue, Royal Academy, London 1972.

Victorian Church Art, exhibition catalogue, Victoria and Albert Museum, London 1952.

Vienna Secession: Art Nouveau 1897–1970, exhibition catalogue, Royal Academy, London 1971.

PERIODICALS

Brooks, H. Allen, Robert W. Winter and David Gebhard, articles in the *Journal of the Society of Architectural Historians*, Vol. 30, No. 4, 1971.

Crow, Gerald H. 'William Morris, Designer', *The Studio*, special number, Winter 1934.

Day, Lewis F. 'William Morris and his Art', *Art Journal*, Easter art annual, 1899.

Floud, Peter 'Dating Morris Patterns', *Architectural Review*, CXXVI, 1959 pp. 14–20.

Holme, C. (ed.) 'Modern Design in Jewellery and Fans', *The Studio*, special number, Winter 1901/2.

Koch, Robert 'American Influences Abroad, 1886 and later', *Journal of the Society of Architectural Historians*, May 1959.

The Studio, first issue 1893.

Wilde, Oscar 'The Soul of Man under Socialism', *Fortnightly Review*, February 1891.

COLLECTED PAPERS

Billcliffe, Roger *J. H. MacNair in Glasgow and Liverpool*, Annual report and bulletin, Walker Art Gallery, Liverpool, Vol. 1 1970–1.

Clark, Robert Judson *Aspects of the Arts and Crafts Movement in America*, Record of the Art Museum, Princeton University, Vol. 34, No. 2, 1975.

Daniel Pabst — Philadelphia Cabinet-maker, Museum bulletin, Philadelphia Museum of Art, Vol. 73, No. 316, April 1977.

Durrant, Stuart *Aspects of the Work of Dr. Christopher Dresser 1834–1904, Botanist, Designer and Writer*, unpublished thesis, Dept. of General Studies, Royal College of Art, June 1973.

Mackmurdo, A. H. *The History of the Arts and Crafts Movement*, and *Autobiographical Notes*, unpublished typescripts, William Morris Gallery, Walthamstow, London.

Thomson, Paul (ed.) *Design, 1860–1960*, Victorian Society, Sixth Conference Report 1970.

PHOTOGRAPHIC ACKNOWLEDGEMENTS

Figures refer to illustration numbers

We would like to thank the following institutions and photographers for making their work available for publication: Great Britain: Bath, American Museum in Britain 13; Craft Study Centre, Holborne of Menstrie Museum 51; Brighton, Art Gallery and Museums (Duncan McNeil photo) 150; Cheltenham, Museum and Art Gallery 44, 50, 51, 53, 215; East Grinstead, Standen 11, 12, 152, 207; Glasgow, T.R. Annan (photographer) 247-9, 262; School of Art Collection 231, 240-2; University, Hunterian Art Gallery 42, 232, 238; Harrow, Kodak Museum 264; Leicester, Museums and Art Gallery 187, 212-4; London, Victor Arwas Collection 298; Bethnal Green Museum 93, 95, 206; A.C. Cooper (photographers) 11, 12, 37, 38, 59, 60, 77, 105, 148, 152, 207, 239, 311; Richard Dennis Ltd, 39, 106, Editions Graphiques 104, 172, 203, 268, 296, 297, 300-2, 309; Fine Art Society 36, 55, 132, 161, 201, 239, 244, 259, 261; Howard Grey (photographer) 44, 50, 52, 69; Haslam & Whiteway 7, 24, 25, 32, 69, 76, 81, 83, 85, 86, 130, 131, 327; Ken Jackson (photographer) 93, 95, 206; John Jesse Ltd. 164; Graham Kirkland (photographer) 24, 25, 32; National Monuments Record 71, 82, 102, 103, 183, 199, 200; Phillips Fine Art Auctioneers 17, 18, 114, 122, 157, 210, 211, 280, 282; Royal Academy (Charles Handley-Read Collection) 15, 16, 156, 185, 266, 292; Sotheby's Belgravia Ltd 21-3, 28, 61-3, 68, 88-90, 94, 97, 99, 101, 112, 113, 124, 234, 235, 246, 265, 267, 270, 272, 273, 277-9, 333; Victoria and Albert Museum, front cover, frontispiece, 1, 3-5, 8, 26, 35, 41, 49, 54, 56-8, 66, 67, 72-4, 78, 79, 84, 87, 91, 92, 125-9, 135-9, 146, 147, 149, 151, 154, 158-60, 163-71, 173-8, 184-6, 188, 192, 195, 196, 202, 223, 236, 237, 243, 245, 250, 263, 269, 271, 274, 281, 283-91, 293-5, 299, 314, 334; Wartski Ltd 193; B. Weinreb (Architectural Books) 257; William Morris Gallery, Walthamstow 6, 10, 37, 45, 46, 59, 60, 70, 77, 80, 140-5, 148, 153, 155; Christopher Wood Ltd 38, 105, 311; Perth, City Art Gallery 204; United States: Buffalo, Albright-Knox Art Gallery 27, 253; Chicago, Art Institute 9, 230, 254, 255; Historical Society 117, 120; School of Architecture Foundation 9; Monterey, Morley Baer (photographer) 19, 43, 47, 48, 304-6, 308, 316-23, 326; Newark, Art Museum 98, 111, 224-7; New York, Antiques Magazine 14, 189; Brooklyn Museum 121; Cooper-Hewitt Museum of Design 116, 328, 329; Metropolitan Museum of Art 118, 229, 256, 258; Taylor & Dull Inc. (photographers) 33, 98; Jordan Volpe Gallery 20, 34, 100, 190, 216-22, 313; Todd M. Volpe Collection 33, 194; Oakland, Art Museum 307, 310, 330-2; Philadelphia, Museum of Art 29, 107, 109, 218; Princeton, University Art Museum 31, 96, 115, 123, 208; Syracuse, Everson Museum of Art 324; University City, Museum 325; Washington, Smithsonian Institution 108, 110, 228; Winter Park, Rollins College, McLean Collection 303; Private Owners 119, 191, 198, 205, 209, 252, 312.

INDEX